HANNAH: FROM DACHAU TO THE OLYMPICS AND BEYOND

With Best Wishes
Jean Messinger

HANNAH

From Dachau
to the Olympics
and Beyond

Jean Goodwin Messinger

White Pelican Press
Windsor

ABOUT THE AUTHOR

Jean Goodwin Messinger has a variety of interests and endeavors in her background including writing and lecturing about historic architecture, teaching high school English and college art history, and a life-long hobby as a fiber arts collector and craftsperson. In addition to writing, she guides other people in recording their personal and family histories. Her present passions are seven grandchildren, gardening, and living in beautiful Colorado.

Other works:

Pride, Prejudice, and Politics: The History of El Paso County's 1903 Courthouse

A Closer Look at Beaver Dam

Faith in High Places (co-author)

Where Thy Glory Dwells (co-author)

Copyright 2005 by White Pelican Press
Second Printing 2009
All rights reserved
White Pelican Press, PO Box 455, Windsor, Colorado 80550

Library of Congress Catalog Card Number 2005926382
ISBN 0-615-12866-1

Cover and book design by Full Circle Marketing & Design

TABLE OF CONTENTS

DEDICATION

To 145 children who haven't survived
And to one who has

To all children everywhere
Who trust the rest of us to love them, care for them,
And guide them to productive independence
Without fear, neglect, and abuse

Begging their forgiveness
When we fail to meet their expectations
Or to keep the promises made to them when we bring them
into this world

Hannah's Dedication

To Karen my doctor and best friend, who walks, runs, and skis
with me, and keeps me alive. Thank you so much.

To Mark, who lost a mother and gained a new mother. I lost
a son and gained a new son. Thank you so much.

ACKNOWLEDGMENTS

Thank you most of all to Hannah for the sometimes difficult hours spent recalling and sharing those personal episodes of tragedy and triumph.

Tom for his patience, enthusiasm, sharing his opinions (whether solicited or not), reading the manuscript, and cooking dinner now and then.

Gloria Petersen for bringing Hannah and me together. Without Gloria, none of this would have happened.

Readers Earl Glosser, Mary Jane Rust, Rea Ann Trotter, Prof. Barry Rothaus, and Lorna Knowlton for their editing expertise and especially for their honesty.

The always helpful, patient, and knowledgable staff of the Windsor-Severance Library for mountains of research materials they made available through interlibrary loan: Suzy Cramer, Judy Hergert, Sharon Jeffryes, Pam Parish, Melissa Martin-Powell, Bev Reule, Karen Weatherly, Darlene Willis, Karen Johnson, Rea Ann Trotter, and Carol Engel, library director.

Channing Meyer, graphic artist supreme of Full Circle

Marketing and Design in Loveland, for always thinking outside the box—in layout, cover, and all things that required originality and creativity.

Sara Jane Snyder for bailing me out when the computer fought back.

Veterans of the 42nd Rainbow Division and of the 45th Thunderbird Division of the Seventh Army of the US, who tried to help me verify accounts of the Dachau Liberation. They were there: Brig. Gen. (Ret.) Felix Sparks, Sid Shafman, Jack Hallowell, and Dee R. Eberhart.

Dr. Barbara Distel, Director of the Dachau Memorial Site, for clarifying general information.

Maren Read, Photo Research Coordinator/Archivist at the US Holocaust Memorial Museum in Washington, D.C., and Michlean Amir, Reference Archivist at the museum.

INTRODUCTION

A Holocaust survivor managing a national chain motel in an all-American-type community in northern Colorado is a surprising discovery. At age 67, Hannah is the last known survivor of a group of 146 children rescued from the German concentration camp at Dachau by American forces in April of 1945.

She has not been recorded before and only began talking about her experience within the last decade, after she came to America and could comfortably identify herself as a Jew. A modest and personable lady, Hannah doesn't present herself as a victim or professional Holocaust survivor. She tells her story when asked, describing gripping details of the horrific existence that aborted her childhood. Then, by the time she wows listeners with the accomplishments as well as tragedies of her personal life since 1945, the camp experience becomes almost (but not seriously) an *"Oh, by the way . . ."* appendage.

Hannah's narrative is unusual within the body of Holocaust literature. First of all, most children did not survive long in the camps; they weren't allowed to. When I became acquainted with Hannah, and as she unfolded her story, I was struck by the humility with which she repeatedly sought to explain her own survival. *"Why was I allowed to survive?"* *"God must have had a purpose for me."* *"Why am I still here?"* *Survive* is a word that comes up frequently in her speech as well as in the writings of other Holocaust recorders. Hannah doesn't see her survival as a passive, random happening. How much was luck, how much was her own determination, how much was divine intervention, no one will ever know.

Many of those 145 children took their demons to the grave. To speak for them is a noble endeavor, even obligation, that honors their memory. In addition, Hannah is finding the purpose she has sought. It was not an easy one to fulfill. This is not an account of the Holocaust, however. What is written here is about Hannah herself. For her entire life is a tribute to tenacity, courage, resilience, and the power of faith—words used to describe every survivor's memoirs.

Detailed Holocaust accounts have been written by many survivors, and there are similarities as well as differences between them. The Holocaust itself has been a rich subject for psychologists as well as historians and biographers. At any rate, if you have read the abundant literature, toured associated sites or visited relevant museums, you have an idea of the horror of those times. For some survivors, it has taken many years to reach the point of being willing or able to articulate their experiences. But with the passage of time, perspectives do change, memories lighten their grip, and embarrassment and anger change to pride.

What you are about to read is the story of Hannah, a German Jew who spent her childhood from age three to nearly eight, without her parents, in the camp at Dachau. Because she was interned at such a young age, she fortunately does not have total recall of that experience, but certain elements of it are still vivid.

For most of us, memory does not reach back as far as the fourth year. However, if you have been a parent or pre-school teacher of a three-year-old, you have a pretty clear idea of what being a three-year-old is all about. In fact, you probably have a better understanding than the child himself does. With that perspective, a reader will be more sickened about Hannah's brutal treatment and more distressed over what she missed in her dehumanized childhood: cuddling and kisses at bedtime, ice cream, stuffed animals, band-aids on "owies," being read to, cousins and grandparents, birthday parties, trips to the zoo. . .

But Hannah didn't miss those things because she didn't know they existed. To be sure, there are millions of children all over the world today who lack such "basics." Hannah and the children confined with her lacked the basics pet-owners consider essential for their dogs.

Although the years in camp were in many ways her defining years, that ordeal is not the focus of this narrative. It is a starting point that makes everything that follows even more remarkable. Nor is this a sad story. There are sad elements in it— episodes that will break your heart. Keep in mind, however, as Hannah does, that she has met those challenges and overcome their devastating effects. They are in the past, done with, let go. Nothing can change what happened, her losses can never be recovered, and she accepts that.

The lady who stands tall before you has not one person living she can call family. She doesn't know what her parents looked like, or what she looked like as a baby or young child.

She lives in an adopted but alien country she doesn't know well or understand completely, trying to connect anew. She often finds this new challenge incompatible with her values, expectations, and definitions. Under those conditions it is not easy to form meaningful relationships. Yet she loves America and being American, and she is grateful to be in the U.S.

Hannah's odyssey is presented from dialogues between two people who learned a lot from each other during many hours of interviews that took place over several months. I have quoted her as she expressed herself on audio-tape. Readers will find her unedited idiom clear enough and often charming. Although she knows several languages, she was not comfortable enough with English to write an autobiography. In my opinion, however, a story like this one has more impact and credibility when presented from an outsider's point of view, because the telling should be more objective. As the narrative unfolds, however, the author's prejudices are apparent.

We discussed diverse topics from death, international relations, and religion, to American elections and the lasting effects of sexual abuse. Some issues were too personal or sensitive to share here, but always there was honesty. Hannah admits to being direct, even undiplomatic. I also found a sense of humor and feistiness that make entirely plausible her personal conquests and accomplishments. It isn't difficult to imagine what a spunky little cuss she must have been as a youngster.

My purpose in publishing Hannah's story is to remind readers one more time of the power of the human spirit to overcome adversity. May you be strengthened as you too learn some important life lessons from this child of Dachau.

Dachau is about ten miles northwest of Munich.

Interned children. Courtesy of United States Holocaust Memorial Museum.

PART I
Chapter One

FROM DARKNESS INTO LIGHT

"One gets accustomed to what is."
— *Hannah*

Hannah was three years old when everything that was hers in her short life was taken from her. Even her identity. For many years she didn't know her real name. Only the number 3445 tattooed on her tiny left arm distinguished her from #3444 and #3446. She couldn't read those peculiar markings nor could she understand the strange (German) words barked at her by grown-up bullies, dressed alike and carrying guns.

Hannah was the name given to her at birth. It sounded too Jewish in Germany of the 1930s, and so it was exchanged by her family for a more acceptable, safer, Teutonic name. That accommodation did not spare her or her family from the fate that awaited them delivered by their own countrymen determined to exterminate every Hannah, Aaron, and Rebecca from the face of the earth.

Our Hannah was born in Mainz-on-the-Rhine in 1938 while her parents were attending a medical conference there. Both parents were physicians in Berlin, prosperous and respected members of their community. They each had emigrated from St. Petersburg as children in 1914 when the situation for Jews in Russia had become "uncomfortable." From 1933-38 Jews were leaving Germany for the same reasons and were officially urged to do so. Hannah's family, however, did not want to go through resettlement again. It was a move not to be taken lightly—finding a country that would give them refuge, leaving their property and livelihood behind, and essentially starting over. Although the situation for Jews in Germany was becoming increasingly dangerous, Hannah's parents counted on their usefulness as physicians to exempt them from serious persecution. Logic would suggest that to be a reasonable conclusion. But these were not reasonable times. By the time the situation became obviously critical, it was too late.

Hannah's paternal grandparents, also physicians, lived close by; the two families' houses were separated by a common garden. Both sets of grandparents had been friends in St. Petersburg, had emigrated to Germany together, and originally lived next door to each other. Hannah's maternal grandparents died when Hannah's mother was about eighteen years old.

I don't know what they died of or if they are buried in Berlin. I never could find out. Then my dad married my mother. That was probably the easiest way, as they grew up together.

This information was acquired after the war from civil records and from later visits to Hannah's old neighborhood in Berlin. It is the extent of genealogical affirmation about her family. Holocaust memoirs often begin with pages of identification and descriptions of family members, relationships, occupations, and accomplishments— portraying an idyllic pre-war family life and often illustrated with photographs. Hannah has none of that.

She describes the night in 1941 when her world changed.

I heard something very hard and loud banging on the door. It sounded like someone kicking the door in. They were soldiers with guns, shouting and screaming. I was crying. I wanted to take my teddy bear along, but they wouldn't allow that. The next thing I know is we were in the box car (presumably going to Dachau, about seven hours from Berlin). *I remember that it smelled terrible, people all over, some lying down. At the time I didn't know they were dead. I had to throw up all the time, no bathroom, and terrible smell.*

Descriptions by other Holocaust survivors who were trans-
ported to the camps in this way reveal these same conditions.
The cars were jam-packed, standing room only, cold or suffocat-
ingly hot, no food or water, no privacy or facilities for natural
elimination processes—for hours and hours, even days. The
anxiety from uncertainty must have been as excruciating as the
physical discomfort.

*I don't remember if it was my mother who held me those
seven hours; I suppose it was. When we got to the camp
we were separated, and there was no one to hold on to
anymore.*

Three years old and *there was no one to hold on to anymore*—
not until liberation came four years later. Hannah never saw her
parents or grandparents again. Well-kept Nazi documents recovered after the war recorded that they all died of heart attacks
on specified dates. This was a common "cause of death" certifi-
cation in the camps. In reality, gas chambers, hanging, gunshot,
starvation, disease, overwork, and physical brutality were the
likely and deliberate agents for inmates' expiration.

What Hannah learned later about her parents and grandparents' disappearance is only part of the story. In the eyes
of anti-Semites, the Jewish problem in Germany contained a
strong racial component. In addition to Jews being considered
lazy, Bolshevistic, war-mongering, and in control of the world's
finances, race injected an irreversible, biological "given." The
latter rationalized the necessity for ridding society of their con-
taminating presence in the gene pool. This policy received attention and acceptance early in the Nazi Regime, in the 1930s,
although strong anti-Semitism existed in Germany long before
Adolph Hitler came along.

Implementing Nazi policy of perfecting the German population by sterilizing or euthanizing those who weakened the purity of German stock required the services of medical practitioners. The first to be targeted were not specifically Jewish, rather the mentally deficient, homosexuals, gypsies, and biologically imperfect. Jews were also labeled among the unfit, undesirable, even dangerous elements within an Aryan-only society. Therefore, Jewish doctors had to be excluded from this campaign of expunction. Some were used later in the camps, however, for other purposes.

On the other hand, large scale elimination of the Jewish population itself did not require medical expertise of attending physicians. True, doctors in white coats were present to "make selections" from among Jews and non-Jews alike. Selection meant a wave of a hand sent individuals to the left to the gas chamber or to the right for a slave labor assignment. Capricious spontaneous judgments were made in determining a subject's fitness for work, based on the subject's condition and appearance at that moment. Prisoners were known to pinch their cheeks or rub something onto them to give them color, in order to present a healthier-looking countenance. Criteria as well as results were arbitrary at best. Stories abound describing heart-rending separations of family members, while at the same time "salvation" often came about from cheating the Devil only by chance.

Nazification of the medical profession in Germany was not without complications. A sizable percentage of German doctors were Jewish—half in many large cities and 13% in the country as a whole. The percentage of Jews in the population was considerably smaller than the numbers they contributed to the medical profession. Nazis early placed restrictions on these Jewish practitioners. They were discredited by their colleagues, disbarred from professional societies, forbidden to care for non-Jewish patients, and generally eliminated from the "competition." At the same time, non-Jewish physicians were prohibited from treating Jews. Consequently, eliminating the services of Jewish doctors was to put a strain on medical care available to the general population, especially as the war lengthened.*

By 1941 when Hannah's family was taken, it is likely her parents and grandparents had already experienced some of this ominous discrimination. No question their services were needed, which they assumed would be their salvation. But a twisted assessment of their worth sacrificed a valuable resource to the demonic ideology of their government. There are other stories told of businessmen and professionals making similar, self-destructive assumptions.

There may have been a reason why Hannah's family was taken to Dachau and not somewhere else. That destination may have saved Hannah's life, as she was apparently a suitable subject for medical experiments on children. Had it been otherwise, they all might have met their destruction immediately and together. What transpired during the few weeks her parents and grandparents remained alive in a different part of the camp can only be speculated. Anxiety over the fate of their three-year-old Hannah must have been devastating to them all.

The next thing I remember is that I was crying all the time. One of the guards told me not to cry anymore. They took us outside to wash in a trough like those used to feed cattle. It was winter and freezing and everyone was crying. There were a lot of soldiers around us. They told us not to cry; they showed us their pistol. They shot a little

---

*For further reference consult Robert Jay Lifton: *The Nazi Doctors: Medical Killing and the Psychology of Genocide*. See Consulted Works.

girl and a little boy next to me in their temple. I was covered in blood. That was the last time I ever cried. I did not understand death at that moment, only that I had to wash the blood off in ice cold water. I don't know how old I was then.

It wouldn't take a psychologist long to analyze why Hannah has not been able to cry since that experience. Her survival depended on it. As her story unfolds, she will demonstrate extraordinary self-control as tragedy after tragedy pummeled her throughout her mature life.

We were ages three to about nine years old, I learned later. At the time, I didn't know how old I was. We lived in a large barracks, boys and girls together, so modesty was unknown. They kept a light on to keep an eye on everybody. Bunkbeds were four sometimes five-deep against the wall. At times we slept two to four kids in one bed.

Clothing was standard striped prison garb often seen in contemporary camp photos. As children wore out their uniform, they would appropriate a deceased child's clothing or receive castoffs from adult inmates. No doubt small sizes were not available for young children, and they likely wore clothes that were several sizes too big for them.

To my query about shoes, Hannah shook her head and gave me that "you-aren't-catching-on-very-quickly" sigh she used on several occasions to emphasize a point. *"We had no shoes."* That seems like a rather superficial comfort item, but in the German climate extremes, on terrain bereft of grass, bare feet would add another discomfort to the children's misery. When children entered the camp, they were stripped, and that included shoes. *"I wonder why my feet were not frozen, and my nose and face."* Viktor Frankl, in his account of his own camp experiences,* describes how shoes were distributed to (adult) inmates—shoes that didn't fit. Worn without socks, the resulting discomfort, even pain, could be as insufferable or worse than wearing no footgear at all.

We got hard dark bread with hot water once a day.* There was no lunch or dinner. Sometimes we ate dirt. Breakfast consisted of loaves of bread thrown into the barracks. Inmates scrambled for their share and hoarded what they didn't eat on the spot by hiding it under their bunks to eat later. Most of the time we put some of the bread under our straw mattresses. There were fights over this bread. The younger ones had to watch out to try to keep food for themselves. During the years I was there I learned to put my food into cracks in the barracks so I would have food if I needed it.

Sometimes when we were outside standing by the fence supposedly getting fresh air, townspeople would try to give us food when the guards weren't looking. You bet they were in danger of being shot, and they were taking a big chance. There were lots of people imprisoned in that camp, and they could see that the people in charge weren't feeding all of us. They saw how skinny we were. I was always afraid to take that bread. I lived by the rules. You learn to live by the rules so nothing will happen to you.

Drinking water was so scarce Hannah used to dip a corner of her towel into the outside trough used for bathing and laundry, to suck on later to help quench chronic thirst.

*Viktor Frankl: *Man's Search for Meaning* See Consulted Works.
* Bread is described in other memoirs as containing sawdust for filler.

Sometimes bouillon was available. What water or liquid nourishment was available was foul-tasting, like sulphur. I always wondered if it had something in it to make us sleep.

Naturally sanitary conditions were appalling. Laundry was done by the children for themselves, infrequently to be sure, and in the only source of water—the trough outside the barracks. While a uniform was drying, its owner went naked. In the big picture, a world without Kleenex and bathroom tissue seems a trivial complaint but a need nevertheless. Leaves and newspapers, when available, answered to that need. Maintenance of the barracks was the responsibility of the children, and a broom and bucket of water met the standard. Barracks were not heated in winter.

These Jewish children spoke Hebrew instead of German, which created some communication problems with their captors. But with a gun pointed at them, ready to be used with little provocation, the children managed to follow orders. There were no female guards, and none of the custodial force, including medical personnel, showed the children any softness. For example, each morning, summer and winter—probably early because it was dark—someone would burst into the barracks shouting at the children to get out of bed and go outside to wash in the troughs of cold water. Sometimes guards had to chisel ice from this "bath" water. Did someone stand over the children to make sure they bathed? Hannah's description would satisfy the dream of every ten-year-old boy who hates to be dragged to the bathtub.

Most of the time I didn't wash. There was nobody there watching. Bodies and clothes were sprayed each morn-

23

ing with little effect. There were bugs everywhere in the barracks, not just lice—on the wall, in our beds, on us. We were bitten by bedbugs and who knows what else.

Camp personnel were less interested in cleanliness than in controlling lice. Another way lice were eliminated was by being eaten by the starving children. The lice problem was reported throughout the camps and was a cause of typhus that ran rampant among the inmates in general. Fear of disease sometimes kept guards at a distance from the barracks.

We were assigned different jobs at the camp. After breakfast we were ordered into line to go to the ovens. When a guard touched you with his stick, you went to work. It was dark when the day started and dark when we finished. The younger ones cut the dead people's hair off. After they came out of the ovens, we removed gold from the teeth of the dead with pliers and hammers.

If Hannah had been older, she might have wondered each time she went to her assignment if she would come face to face with . . . It is too monstrous to contemplate.

Smoke from the ovens where they burned the bodies caused a black cloud and smelled something like propane gas. The smell of the burning bodies cannot be described. The smell of Dachau is the worst memory. I have that smell of the dead and the gas to this day. We also had to remove bones from the warm ovens. We put those into a hole with all the other bodies.

Ash from the crematorium was often processed and marketed as fertilizer. The odor of death is something all camp witnesses report. During war criminal trials held by American military authority at Dachau months after the war ended, that odor was still present.

I remember the adults in their striped uniforms, like us. Some could not walk anymore; some only crawled. We were separated from them by a fence, but we could hear their screams and cries. Always the guns would put an end to the crying.

Tuberculosis, diphtheria, polio, typhus, and hepatitis also occurred in camp, and little Hannah did not escape her share of illness. In addition to disease and mistreatment that ended many lives, many children starved.

They might die during the night, and the next morning the guards would remove their bodies. The camp authority really wanted the kids to die themselves. They just didn't get around to killing us outright for the most part.

Why were these children kept alive? They served other unspeakable purposes besides performing gruesome tasks on cadavers.

Several times a week the guards would come into the bar-racks, choose some of us, gave us chocolate and then sexu-ally abused us in a room in another part of the camp. I remember one boy who was always trying to save me and would stand in front of my bed. He would say, 'Take me, take me.' He may have wanted the chocolate. One day they came in. I was about seven, and they did not take me. They took him instead and he never came back. I think he saved my life that day. I don't remember his name, but I still see his face clearly.

This seems like the most revolting perversion of all, visited upon emaciated, sick, lice-covered young bodies as untouchable as barnyard animals. It was the lure of chocolate that induced the victims to submit to this abuse, but of course they had no choice.

Another use for which the children served conveniently because they were disposable, was for medical experimentation.* Hannah describes always feeling sick while she was in the camp.

> *They regularly took us to the medical center and gave us shots. I didn't know what they were and was never able to find out. I just know they performed medical experiments on some of us. We were always itching, we had scabs all over our bodies, we were dirty and smelled bad. Years later after I returned from Israel, I went back to Dachau and talked to people who lived around there. I asked them why they thought we were spared. My impression was that they had a big experimental thing going on with Jewish kids, and that's why they kept us alive. It was explained to me later that it involved specific ages and special-looking children, and they couldn't do much with the older kids, the teenagers. They needed to have smaller kids to do this. I was too young to understand what they were doing or to ask anything. If somebody had told me, I wouldn't understand anyway.*

Dachau was the center of several kinds of odious experiments, which was brought out in the war criminal trials conducted there in 1945. Not the subject to be analyzed in detail here, my own inquiries to physicians have indicated that some revelations about medical experiments at certain camps were kept confidential by Allied authorities. Secrecy was necessary

---

*Documentation is lacking, but Hannah's position is very firm about this.

in order to keep certain data out of the hands of those who would use the results for harmful purposes.

Although many of Hannah's fellow internees did not survive the harshness and deprivation of camp life, they were not sought out as a group for extermination. In general, children did not survive in the other camps. At Terezin in Czechoslovakia, for example, over 15,000 children entered; 100 survived.*

Individual guards and soldiers had their own barbaric way of killing infants and toddlers, often in the presence of their mothers. Those children younger than fifteen were quickly eliminated. They were usually moved into the gas chambers very soon after arrival. There were cases where younger teens were able to pass themselves off as being older than they really were, therefore useful as slave labor and avoiding immediate death in the gas chambers.

In many camps, survivors of all ages were sometimes individuals who hadn't been interned for long. However, the Jews of Hungary entered the camps in 1944, late in the war, and were immediately gassed. Russian troops reached the Eastern camps early in 1945, several weeks before Dachau prisoners were rescued by American troops. Every day lost before liberation meant thousands didn't make it to freedom.

By the time I was 7 ½ I could not walk any more, could not crawl. I could not eat or drink any more. I was covered with lice and sprayed every day. It must have been right before we were freed or they wouldn't have put up with

---

*See *I Never Saw Another Butterfly* . . . a book of children's drawings and poems from Terezin 1942-1944. See Consulted Works. (The German name for this camp was Theresienstadt.) The originals were seen by author when they were displayed in the Judaic Pavilion at Montreal's Expo 1967. A musical work by Charles Davidson has been composed with this same name, using poems from the book. It is performed by children's choirs.

such a sick person. When they freed us, I weighed twenty-five pounds. My rib cage looked like someone took their hand and pushed it in. There was a big hole in there.

I didn't know how old I was until after we were let out. I didn't know my name was Hannah. I knew myself as Rosemarie, the non-Jewish name my parents gave me later. If you asked me my name when I was three, I would have told you Rosemarie. The other kids in the camp called me Rosemarie. The guards never called us anything. They didn't know or care our names.

Anyway, it was better not to show yourself or do something that the guards would know you were there. What you learn is that you always stand in a crowd, and you never wanted to be seen.

Safety in anonymity is a strategy commonly described in other internee memoirs, demeaning as it was. Anonymity can take other forms, too. There was no sense of time in terms of weeks and months, which blended endlessly, although the cycle of seasons was apparent. A day was defined by its easily perceived routine repeated day after day, month after month, year after year. For her first years of internment, Hannah wasn't aware of a war going on, that her situation was related to that war, and that some day the war would be over. She had no idea of the outside world, or that there was a better life on the other side of the barbed wire that defined hers.

With that narrow perspective, it is difficult to understand why a young child would have any will at all to continue such a harsh and meaningless existence. Viktor Frankl sought to explain that phenomenon in light of his own camp experience as an adult among adults at Auschwitz. Frankl was an Austrian Jew and a psychiatrist, noted today for his theories on psychotherapy. His popular *Man's Search for Meaning* published in 1946 describes how the superhuman survival effort exhibited by some inmates seemed to relate to their having a goal, a purpose in life beyond internment. He witnessed a number of inmates who died fairly healthy, who simply gave up, while others lived the camp experience at death's door for several years. Frankl concluded that those individuals who had a strong desire to live for some purpose could translate that successfully into a hopeful determination to survive. Of course will was not the only controlling factor in the face of numerous dangers faced every minute of every day as a prisoner in one of the camps.

Little Hannah was only conscious of living from one "meal" to the next. Her goal— to have something to eat. So very young, her concept of cause and effect was limited. She understood what the man's shiny thing could do, and she did her best to avoid provoking its use. Her perceptions and strategies were simple, but adequate in the end. What about the behavior of the other children interned with her? She was pretty young to be sensitive to much of that, and probably it was not an issue that would have lasted in her memory after so many years.

I didn't pay a whole lot of attention to the reactions of other kids. I had enough to deal with my own troubles. We didn't have a lot of behavior choices. You either did what you were supposed to or else . . . and you quickly learned that. Some kids just kind of withered and vegetated. They didn't leave their bunk unless they were forced to. As children died, more entered the camp. They were closer to my age, not as young as I was when I came there. Since I was more 'experienced,' I kind of took some of those new kids under my wing, sort of mothered them.

The noises from afar were assumed by the children to be thunder. As Liberation Day approached, bombing increased and came closer. This brought explosions and lights different from the thunder and lightening with which they were familiar. Explosions were also accompanied by a piercing hissing sound. The bombing has been described as sounding like the siren of a police car. Hannah still finds sirens unsettling.

The official liberation of Dachau is recorded as April 29, 1945. More details about the takeover and the camp itself are recounted later in the book.

I remember that day very well. We were sitting outside the barracks, because in the daytime we weren't allowed to stay in there. The guards were yelling and running, and we didn't know what was going on.

Liberation is described similarly at other sites, but in some instances inmates greeted the day in silence, as the garrison had already fled approaching Allied troops during the night. Jack Mandelbaum relates in his memoirs that inmates were locked in their barracks by the deserting guards.* Freedom Day for Dachau inmates was not so simple.

Then American soldiers came into our section of the camp. They also had guns. The children were stand-off-ish at first, suspicious of more uniforms and guns. No one cried. They put us into trucks, and we were not happy about that. We knew we had a little hot water and bread,

*Andrea Warren: *Surviving Hitler: A Boy in the Death Camps.* See Consulted Works.

and we wanted to keep that. Someone carried me out to
a green truck and took me to a hospital near Munich. A
month later I became eight years old.

Several of Hannah's fellow inmates did not survive long after
liberation. For them and for thousands of others, deliverance
came too late. Some accounts of liberating the camps describe
how well-meaning GIs immediately gave some of their rations to
the starving inmates. This often caused them to die. Unprepared
for the horror facing them, soldiers didn't know that medical expertise is required to properly reintroduce nourishment to starving individuals. As a result, these additional tragedies created
a great burden of guilt, that after surviving such an ordeal an
internee would succumb to an innocent act of charity.

Life was to change dramatically for the 146 children rescued
from Dachau, safely and comfortably recuperating in a nearby
German hospital. Nevertheless, serious medical problems per-
sisted.

Besides malnutrition, there were still typhus and lice to
deal with. We had a worm in our colon. We had stuff
you never heard of. I used to know this, but it wasn't very
important at the time. The only important thing was that
I was alive.

The nurses taught Hannah to walk again. Real beds had
clean linen and pillows, and each child had his own sleeping
space. Voices were soft and kind and accompanied by smiles.
The children were free to cry, if there had been something to cry
about. These children had to be taught to use a knife and fork
and sit at a table to eat. They didn't know basic grooming procedures like tooth brushing. Hair washing was unknown in the
camp; it was a routine and required part of their toilette in the

hospital. They had to be taught to speak German. Their knowledge at that point consisted only of certain words and phrases like "Stop crying!" "Hurry up!" and "Come here!" Hannah remembers that every bit of food was new to them.

They gave us food to eat we didn't know what to do with. We hid it under our mattresses, afraid it would be taken away. The records show that we were in the hospital for at least six months.

When one by one they were well enough to leave the hospital, what was to become of them? Orphaned in a devastated country that had done its best to destroy them, options at the end of 1945 were few. No one wanted such children, much less that they were Jewish. Help was to come from a surprising corner.

Chapter Two

THE CONVENT

Every day that I live, I thank God.
– Hannah

*O*ne day some funny-looking people showed up, and we had to leave again. I know now they were nuns. They asked us questions in Hebrew, like where would we like to live. We didn't know; I don't think I answered one question. Next thing we were standing outside. Then a bus was coming taking us into the mountains. There was no choice. Nobody was asking us. I was only eight years old and didn't have any feelings about it at the time.

They took us up into the Alps to Par Jesus Convent. My first impression of the convent was a wall and a fence around the convent. I thought this was so sad to see—imprisoned again. The first thing all of us wanted to know was where are we, who are these people with those funny things on their head, and will they also kill us in time?

Ten or fifteen went into the convent when I did. The rest remained in the hospital, some for as long as a year, and they followed later. Some died there; some died in the convent. After a year, 100 of the original 146 were still alive. While we were there at the convent, there were only the Dachau kids. After we left they took in other kids. Later the orphanage was discontinued as the nuns aged, and there were no replacements.

The nuns had not run an orphanage before. They lived at and managed a convent at Brietbrunn, high in the Bavarian Alps near Munich. There they had a winery using grapes imported from a lower elevation, a bakery, and a farm. For their Jewish charges the nuns built a one-room school and provided barracks inside the wall.

Four kids to a room, one side for the girls, one for the boys. We all ate together. When you walked in, there's a nun sitting there, like a concierge. They didn't have an infirmary, just a nurse. Illness and emergencies had to be dealt with somewhere else. Across from the barracks was the school, with benches and tables the nuns built.

They built furniture and raised geese for down to make pillows and feather beds. Beds squeaked a lot; they were iron on a concrete base, with a frame of iron springs. On top of that was a straw mattress that had to be changed every few weeks.

The convent was self-supporting and raised its own food. At high altitudes crops were limited: potatoes, carrots, cabbage, strawberries, etc. Fruit like oranges and bananas were unknown. For meat they took deer from the woods, wild rabbits, and geese, but served no pork because we were Jewish. They raised chickens but not for us to eat, just for eggs—eggs for us and for baking, for bread, and they made their own noodles. They made everything there. Everything was self-contained (sic), even the milk, even butter—ach!—(remembering) butter without salt!

Remember, we didn't have any shoes in the camp. The first shoes I had were when we came into the convent. They gave us those wooden shoes that Dutch people wear. The nuns made them, and every time our foot got bigger they made larger ones. Or the nine-year-old's got passed down to the eight-year-old, and so forth. Every Saturday you got a piece of handmade soap from the nuns and a big scrub brush. You had to put those shoes under water and you had to scrub and clean. They even knitted sox for us, very thick sox.

Sox must have been a real luxury for those once-tender young feet that had long gone totally unprotected.

Hannah went on to explain more about the convent's operation before the Dachau children's arrival, which gave the nuns a different purpose.

I remember there were 181— lots of nuns. What they did, they sewed a lot for people who were poor, and they gave away a lot of the food they made to poor people. They helped a lot in the war when there was leg amputate (sic), *arm amputate. They made those—whatever you call them.*

We had no schooling at the camp, and many children, like me, had never been to school. (Be reminded that even before the war, the Nazis prohibited Jewish children from attending public schools.) *Now we had the responsibility to attend regularly. I remember it was fun going to school seven or eight hours a day. The first thing we learned was Latin, German, and Old Greek. One nun taught German to all the kids; one taught history to everyone, etc. We had every grade in one class* (like an old-fashioned American country school). *So you learned what the older kids were learning. We went from the first grade to the third grade in one year, so we were able to make our graduation at eighteen.*

I always asked a lot of questions. I don't mind embarrassing myself if I don't understand something. Like I still have questions about the American language, and I'll ask. I did the same thing at school. If I didn't know something, there I was saying I don't understand; tell me more about it. I interrupted a lot. I wanted to learn more than what was being presented. I wanted to know from the ground up—why does this happen, why do we go this way and not that way. That may have come from my parents.

They came from Russia to Germany and had to develop themselves in a society they didn't know. They had to be independent and resourceful.

I wondered when Hannah was first aware of what her situation was, that she had parents at one time. She didn't see anybody in the camp with parents. Did the older kids, who would remember their families, ever talk about such things?

No, they never did. The first time I remember being aware of such things was when we first started school, and the subject came up in a classroom. Kids talked about their parents and what they remembered. I just had to say I didn't have any, because I didn't know anybody that was family. It bothers me even today when I go to a doctor's office or to a bank and they want to know my mother's maiden name or what illnesses they had, like did they have heart attacks or diabetes or something.

I explained why they need to do this. She understands, but it means she either has to explain her situation, or she tells them it's none of their business.

I didn't miss them because I didn't know what family was all about until I got to the convent. For me it wasn't important. I never felt a void because I never had them. It was harder on the older kids, like a lot of things were. They understood things like sexual abuse. They knew their parents and had memories of them. In the camp that was my life. That was the only life I knew, and I didn't know any better.

Several months after we left the hospital and started school, they brought us a rabbi. The German government allowed Israel to have diplomatic relations with Germany by that time. The nuns went to the Israeli consulate, told them they had Jewish children, and asked for a rabbi. A rabbi was brought from Israel. He told us who these nuns were, who we were (!!), and that we should go to school and learn. He was like a father to us, held us in his arms, and came to see us every day. We could talk Hebrew again with him, and it felt so good, like we were at home. He left to go back to Israel in 1954 or '55, not long before I left the convent.

The rabbi explained the whole concept of extermination, why Hitler did that and that he wanted a pure race of his own. He told us about our coming from Egypt into Israel, about the Israel state in 1948, and he explained the whole history of the Jewish people. He was trying to give us an understanding that some people don't like us. I always wanted to know more about that. Why don't they like Jewish people? Just because they are workaholics, because they are successful? These aren't good enough reasons for me.

The nuns didn't try to convert us. There was no scripture reading, no prayer, just rituals at sabbath and holidays after the rabbi came. In the camp we knew nothing of Judaism. We were not really aware of our Jewish heritage. I learned my name is Hannah as well as Rosemarie; that's all I knew then. Having a certain name was not part of my consciousness.

The nuns did introduce us to Christmas. They celebrated Christmas on December 24th. They went out in the woods and got a tree. We all took part in that. They got the tree inside, but we never knew where they would put up the tree, because we weren't allowed to look. The tree was only put up by the nuns, because they believe that Kriss Kringle, not Santa Claus, comes on Christmas Eve. Santa Claus has to do with January 6th and has nothing to do with our American Christmas.* Kriss Kringle was a woman angel, and she comes when that tree is up. The door is locked. The angel will put on the candles, bobs, lebkuchen—which is a kind of gingerbread cookie with chocolate frosting—and gingerbread men that the nuns made.

Christmas Eve exactly at five o'clock a bell rang. And we all went into the room where the Christmas tree was; every year it was in a different room. The nuns were standing at the piano singing 'Stille Nacht, Heilige Nacht.' And we all had to participate in having a poem to say. We had to say all those poems before we got to eat, in that same room. What we ate was frankfurters and German potato salad. Every year always the same.

Afterward the nuns gave us each a present. It wasn't wrapped in paper; it was always unwrapped. Each kid got one present. It was usually something to eat, or a scarf, or sox—no toys. After that we went to church. Rather, the nuns went to church, but we were invited, and most of

---

*There is a tradition in America that Kriss Kringle is synonymous with Santa Claus.

39

the time we went along because it was at midnight and we could stay up. Afterwards they would take us on a sleigh ride. The next morning we all gathered around the Christmas tree. We helped make cookies and waited for the goose to cook for dinner. By noon the meal was ready, including red cabbage and potato dumplings. Afterward we had tortes with vanilla cream and butter cream. Every year they did the same. The nuns made a real effort to make the holiday soothing and comfortable for us.

All that was missing from this scene was Julie Andrews.

The nuns were very kind to us, although they never hugged us. The experience there was so positive that I wanted to open an orphanage when I left the convent. Most of the Dachau children were eventually adopted out of the convent orphanage. The nuns wanted us to smile so we would be appealing to those who might adopt us. I never smiled, because I wanted to stay where I was. We had a good home, a bed, plenty of food. For the first time I had my own bed and food every day. We came to them all messed up. There was no counseling available at the convent, and I have never received any. The nuns made human beings out of us. They were our family. I am grateful to my nuns for putting us back together, for putting me where I am today.

Some of the adopted children stayed in Germany; some were taken to Israel by Israeli families. I found out where they were when I left the convent. There were about forty of us who kept in touch through the years. I had a little book where I kept addresses and information about them, when they died, etc.

Because of the war criminal trials after the war, authorities came to the convent seeking identification of German SS troops and other personnel attached to the camp. The children were shown photographs, but Hannah was unable to identify anyone. Nor did she recognize anyone by name. *"They all looked alike to me, and I didn't pay attention to their faces."*

Life at the convent was not without excitement. After the Russians took over Berlin, Hannah participated in a cold-war drama worthy of John le Carre.

At first after the war it was hard to get in and out of Berlin. The only way was on the train. Those trains were always crowded, because people were coming in and out of Berlin looking for their lost relatives. Some nuns were trying to get to our convent near Munich. They had got caught in Berlin by the war and couldn't get out because of the Russians. So our nuns took it on themselves to go to Berlin to try to get them out the best way they could. To do that, they took along seven or eight of us kids.

We took a train from the convent to a certain place. It was a big thing for us to go train-riding. It's about seven or eight hours on the train. All of a sudden, after hours of being on that train, the train stopped. We got off and we started to walk. You had to walk through a gravel pit in order to get over the border where there weren't any Russians. In order to do that, these nuns had to have children with them so they wouldn't be killed by the Russians.

We were half way through that gravel pit, and there up on top was a Russian guard. I hear him still in my ears. When I think about it I can't hardly believe this happened to us. He shouted, 'Stoi!' That means 'halt' in Russian,

41

and the nuns didn't even acknowledge that, like they didn't understand. No, it wasn't all right to be there, and it was a very dangerous thing to do. The nuns thought that if they got caught, they would tell the Russians these children had to go to Berlin to their parents, in order to explain what we were doing there. And that they didn't have any money to go farther on the train. You see, you could go all the way to Berlin on the train, but the Russians would want to see your passport, and we didn't have one. So that one Russian with someone else as an interpreter stood right in front of us with his gun pointing at us in that gravel pit. We were scared to death. I didn't know why they were putting us through that.

As we came to Berlin, we found out. It was Mother Superior who was stuck in Berlin.

She belonged to our convent and got trapped in the war over there and couldn't get out. The nuns could only do this with children, because the Russians liked children, and the nuns were counting on them feeling sorry for us. They let us go; otherwise none of us might not still be alive. We only saw one Russian, with a gun, and the interpreter. We were down low in that pit so nobody could see us for a while. There were no cars around there. At a certain spot you crossed into West Berlin. Before that, when you were on the other side, you were in the Russian zone, and you just didn't go there. The nuns knew how dangerous it was; that's why they took us along.

Then we walked back out the same way we got there. We didn't get caught this time, but we were so scared—having someone point a gun at you, and you couldn't understand

*what they were saying. Hearing that 'STOI!' was enough
to make you freeze. But we got away with it and probably
stole some coals and potatoes along the way.*

As for daily life at the convent for the ten years Hannah was
in the nuns' care, the following description gives an idea of the
independence that contributed to her resolve to make it through
the camp experience.

*I was the only one at the convent who was organized
enough to have allowance left over at the end of the
month. The German government provided this allowance
to orphans. I also stashed food that I could bargain away.
I was very self-sufficient and had a lot of self-control.
Those traits had to be developed in the camp in order to
survive, and I was determined to survive. Remember that
crying put a bullet into your head from that shiny thing.
You learned early not to cry.*

*By age nine I was old enough to be given chores to do. We
had regular housekeeping assignments: cleaning, cooking,
maintaining our own space. I was the naughtiest child of
the group. I wouldn't make my bed or work in the kitchen
or work in the fields. If there was a door you shouldn't
open, I'd head straight for that door. I remember well that
I wanted to know why these nuns were dressed like that. I
peeked through the peephole at night and looked to see if
they had hair underneath that whatever you call it. One
day we were playing ball, and I just took my hand and
ripped this thing down, and then I knew!*

*They just understood they couldn't shut me up. The more
they tried, the more I talked. I just wanted to know everything and in detail. I wrote it down in a diary, but I*

don't have that anymore. If you would read my diary, you would understand that I was a bad girl.

Unfortunately she left the diary behind when she went to Israel after she left the convent. Hannah agreed what a valuable resource was lost there. We never understand at the time how important those recordings are.

We were given a choice— to do chores or ski. If you wanted to ski, you could ski all day if you were good at it and be exempt from housekeeping chores. The nuns were very sports-oriented in their thinking. If anybody liked skiing, that became a "chore" for them. The nuns taught us to ski. That was a lot of work to teach those children. And the nuns liked skiing, so naturally they picked something they liked, and they figured out the kids could use that some day. That was a good reason. I remember Sister Elizabeth; she skied with her habit tucked between her legs from behind, brought to the front and fastened under a belt.

There were four of us who wanted to be in sports. There were some kids who didn't want to do sports at all, who preferred to help in the convent and do housework. I was a sports fanatic and later played handball as well as soccer, and I was the first to volunteer to learn to ski. This was an easy choice for me—high in the Alps, lots of snow, beautiful surroundings, but no lifts, no tows. You skied down and carried your skis back up the mountain for the next run. Our skis were wooden and handmade by the nuns. They had to be waxed regularly. I also got a new kind of shoe for skiing; they bought me leather boots to ski in.

From nine and a half-years-old I spent several hours

each day on the slopes, and I did well at it. On Sunday, the one day we didn't have school, we skied all day. We competed against other schools. On one occasion a man was watching us and asked me to show him what I could do. I showed him. Then people from the German Olympic Committee came to watch us ski; they decided on three of us.

At fourteen I was put into the Olympic Village in Munich to prepare for the 1956 Olympics at Cortina in Italy. We trained hard several hours a day, seven days a week, and had school on top of that. There were almost as many kids as at the convent, mostly teen-agers; forty-six were girls. I spent those years from age fourteen to eighteen training and competing for Germany. We were given a month off in summer to go back to the convent and relax. There was one coach for each four or five kids, plus the head coach and his assistant. They were there to correct us, to clock us, etc. And NO, I never got bored with such a regimen. I wanted to be outdoors all the time. That was the big thing for me; traveling wasn't an attraction at that time.

The first place we traveled to out of the country was Zermatt in Switzerland, to the Matterhorn. The Swiss mountains were a whole new experience from the small mountains we skied in Bavaria. That was also my first experience in a hotel, very strange for kids from the convent. If we didn't know the food, we would not touch it.

We also traveled to and competed in New Zealand, Australia, Canada, and several places in the US: Utah,

Colorado, and Sun Valley. Each year we learned more. I broke many pairs of skis but no bones.

Just a few out of the original forty-six girls in the program got chosen for the Olympics. In order to be chosen, you had to get medals and cups from the competitions we entered. They filtered out those who didn't win, shuffled through and eliminated until there were just a few left. These are the best skiers. I was one of those chosen in 1956.

Musical training was also part of life at the convent, and while traveling with the ski team, the children from the convent were able to continue their musical regimen. How did the nuns expose their charges to serious music? Did they have a record player? As isolated as the convent was, they surely weren't attending concerts.

No, but we had to play on that piano, which I didn't like at first. The nun was sitting over here, and the piano was sitting over there, and every time you did a note wrong, well . . . First you learned the notes, then you got to do it on the piano, then you went to the harp, then you could go to the fiddle. We had our days filled.

When Hannah went off with the ski team and traveled part of the time, how did she and other music students keep up their music?

They made sure that where we stayed had access to a piano; the other instruments we could take with us. Because we had school while we were training, we also had music in that school. Each one of us had a private tutor. We always went to a place where they had everything there. For instance, we stayed at a convent in Georgetown, here in Colorado, the same order we had at home—Par Jesus order. We had our skiing, our schooling, everything. We didn't have time to play like other kids did; we never played.

Hannah has described how limited the diet was at the convent because the convent was self-sufficient, and crops were limited due to the high altitude. While traveling internationally they got canned and dried fruit, something like tofu, soy products, and drank soy milk " . . . *because we should have good nutrition.*" Their food was prepared for them, and Hannah ate her first banana at Cortina.

I competed in the 1956 Olympics in downhill and slalom. I won no medals but was proud to participate.

It is noteworthy that a Jew represented Germany just a decade after the Holocaust; however, Hannah was not identified as a Jew. While at Cortina, Hannah met Israelis.

They were skiers, but they didn't have an Olympic ski team at that time. They were at Cortina to teach themselves what an Olympic team was all about, and they weren't a team for quite a while, not until 1964, I think. Nineteen seventy-two was their second time—the year of the massacre of the Israeli team at Munich.

We didn't get any money out of the Olympics. Afterwards we didn't get marketing opportunities like they do today. It was just for pleasure; today it's a whole lot different. By the time it was over, nobody talked about it again. We just went back to normal life.

Christmas celebration in 1957 shortly before Hannah left for Israel. The setting is the Berlin home of the Kappe family, who became acquainted with Hannah as the result of their visits to the convent. They befriended Hannah and included her as part of their Jewish family. They continue to communicate with each other. The Christmas tree was set up especially for Hannah, carrying on the tradition she was accustomed to at the convent. Notice Herr Kappe's missing right arm, a casualty of the war.

Chapter Three

ON HER OWN

If you don't like yourself, you aren't going to like anybody else. You have to like yourself first.
— Hannah

The 1956 Olympics were over, and a new chapter was about to begin for Hannah. At eighteen it was time for her to leave the convent. She was one of two Dachau internees remaining; the other was a boy a year older, not in good health, and he died soon after.

Graduated from the convent high school, upon coming of age Hannah had already determined she would go to Israel. From the nuns she received her personal records retrieved from the camp by American liberating forces, plus a sum of money given to all orphans at eighteen by the German government.

I wanted to see the homeland that was my heritage. They gave us enough money to live on for one year without having to work, so we could get used to the world and being on our own. I also got my first pair of real shoes, that I could walk out of that convent. These were a gift from the nuns, a pair of brown suede lace-up shoes that were the best thing I had ever owned.

Leaving the convent, Hannah was now completely on her own, and she had some scores to settle. She intended to relocate in Israel, but first she wanted to find out what she could about her family and if she could get her parents' property back. She visited Dachau, but there wasn't much to see; it had not yet been turned into a tourist site. She went to the University of Berlin to see if she could study medicine there, and she had the tattoo on her arm removed. Most of these issues weren't resolved until she returned from Israel.

In response to questions about her tattoo removal, she showed me her arm. Skin had been grafted to the spot. She didn't remember the tattooing, which would have been painful to a young child, done without anesthetic and less than tenderly applied.

Before I went to Israel, I went to a hospital and demanded that thing be taken off. I just knew I had to get it off; I could never have lived with that. I would never show it to anyone. It was like what they do to cattle, like you're being led off to slaughter any minute. That's why it was the first thing I did, even before I bought a ticket to Israel.

After World War II the future was uncertain for Jews in Germany as well as in other parts of Europe, and many Jews left the continent. Some came to America. Some opted for what was their spiritual, cultural, and ancestral homeland in Palestine, now Israel. Immediately after the war, however, while the British still controlled Palestine, European Jews were not allowed into the country. That situation changed after 1948 when Israel became an autonomous state.

To participate in building a nation that both welcomed and needed them was appealing to those whose very worth had been denied in such a personal way. For over a generation, even their collective identity had been subjected to the most degrading and false assessment. It would be reassuring, therefore, to enter a hospitable environment that affirmed, cherished, and secured their Judaic heritage. The very idea of acceptance was to be savored. Unfortunately, history has shown that what Israel offered to the Jews was not a panacea. Common ideology wasn't enough to achieve the peace or security they sought.

Hannah took the money she received upon leaving the convent and bought a ticket to Tel Aviv.

I had enough money left over to live on for a whole year, but I didn't have to, so I put it in the bank. I knew ahead that I wanted to serve in the army. When I got off the airplane in Tel Aviv, I went to the immigration office and told them I wanted to stay. I joined the army and they put me into a kibbutz. The army didn't pay much, but we didn't need anything; necessities were provided. Saving that money meant that if I needed to leave because I didn't like it, I could leave. And that's what I did.

Living in a kibbutz is a communistic (sic) *way of life. In a way, Israel is a socialized country—almost. I don't think people in America know exactly what the communistic life style is, what living in a socialized country is all about. Just picture yourself being a soldier. They are all in the barracks, two bunks next to each other, ten or twenty in one barrack, just like Dachau—except for linens and pillows. There's a mess hall and a kitchen. You don't own anything. You are fed by the government. You are working for the government, and you are doing your best to stay alive for that government. You have your little table and bed, and you go out to work. If you had a family, you live in an apartment.*

Kibbutz is where you send your children in order to learn, like a military camp for boys and girls. It's important that you learn to give 50% and to take 50%, and you live in the middle. You have to learn to control your temper. You are very much disciplined. That's how you survive in a socialized community. It isn't bad. I didn't mind living that way, because I did it. I wouldn't want to live my whole life that way, but for a short time it didn't matter.

We learned how to be a soldier. But I told them at the beginning I wouldn't hold or carry a gun. Israel had only been a state for less than ten years since the British left, and there was much building going on. There were no trees, so we planted avocado trees and olive trees—all kinds of trees for people to buy. People from around the world donated money to Israel to plant trees, and then their names would be put on the trees.

Life in Israel did not suit Hannah for several reasons. First of all, she found there were things she didn't like about army life. The regimentation itself brought back unpleasant associations with life in the camp at Dachau.

After you've been raised in a convent, life was too restricted again in the kibbutz. Too confined, too many people eating and sleeping together in one room. It wasn't what I was looking for.

Another detraction from settling in Israel was that she found the political situation too tense. There was unrest, not just with the Palestinians but with other countries who were antagonistic toward the formation of a state of Israel. In addition, she was not comfortable among the Palestinian population.

It wasn't a question of not liking them or not getting along with them personally. I just could not go through another war.

The eastern Mediterranean climate was another difficult adjustment for Hannah. Its steady, bright sunshine was unlike what she was accustomed to. All that went with a desert environment was about as far as one could get from life in the Bavarian Alps.

While I lived in Israel I made many friends in the kibbutz. As young people that was easy to do. But outside, if it wasn't business they didn't want to talk to you, and it wasn't easy to make friends. Later, as an adult when I took tours to Israel, and there were many all over Israel, they didn't accept me as a Jew. They looked on me as a German, not as a Jew, a German bringing people into Israel as tourists.

In Israel Hannah reconnected with several of the convent children who had been adopted by Israelis. These associations remained important as this group reached maturity (if they reached maturity) and scattered to pursue their various choices for education, vocation, and national citizenship. Being in a Jewish environment also allowed Hannah to become Hebrew-speaking again.

I spoke only Hebrew until I was eight, German at the convent until eighteen, and home again to Hebrew. Jewish Israelis speak both Hebrew and Yiddish; Yiddish is just an older form of Hebrew.*

She had signed on to serve in the Israeli army for two years, but at the end of one year Hannah was ready to go back to Berlin.

---

*Yiddish is historically a language of Central and Eastern European Jews, resulting from a fusion of several tongues including old German dialects, Hebrew, Aramaic, Slavic languages, Old French, and Old Italian. (American Heritage Dictionary of the English Language)

Chapter Four

BERLIN

*You should live every minute of every day
of your life to the fullest.*
– Hannah

Back in Berlin, Hannah had an agenda. *"I was looking for an education. I wanted to go into the medical field, and that wasn't available to me in Israel. There were no spaces; money wasn't the issue."* She was easily accepted into the medical program at the University of Berlin, to satisfy a dream to become a physician like her parents. In the German socialized system, advanced education was provided at state expense. Hannah also began a search to find out more about her family and her roots in Berlin.

I traveled to Dachau to find documents about my parents and grandparents. They had a record book that you can look up people; the Nazis kept such complete records on everybody. When the Jews came there they had to give up their identity papers, and that's what they wrote in that book. There's a number, like my number is in that book. Their addresses were in there. I learned that my grandparents were killed about a month after they got there. My parents shortly after that. That is also the time I found out that the German medical professionals at the camp were performing medical experiments on us kids.

In Berlin, Hannah spent time trying to identify the neighborhood and dwellings where her parents and grandparents had lived. At the addresses listed in the Dachau record book, she found two substantial, stylish mansions being occupied by the Chinese and Russian embassies. She knocked on neighborhood doors to ascertain if there were people still living in the neighborhood who could give her information about her pre-war existence. Unlike America, where society is more mobile and people move every few years, the Berlin neighborhood was static, and the same people were still living in the same houses a dozen years after the war, *". . . and will live in those houses until they die,"* according to Hannah. American Mid-Westerners, or wherever there is historically a German immigrant population, can relate to that same willingness to "stay put."

She surprised one elderly lady who occupied a house next door and remembered little Hannah and her family, never expecting to see any of them again. She was a sympathetic resource, and she and Hannah developed a close friendship that continued for several years, until the older woman's death. This relationship provided substantial information about Hannah's past—details that weren't available from the camp records.

I wished someone would have had some pictures, birth certificates, or any of those things, but there was nothing. It's like we never existed except in that book.

It seemed reasonable to Hannah to try to retrieve ownership of the family's two former residences. Obviously there had never been any legal transfer of title. Her efforts through the German government were initially unsuccessful. To evict legitimate international agencies, which these embassies were, would have created an awkward diplomatic situation. Whatever conditions were known at the time their contracts were drawn up can only be surmised. It is likely no one expected these "abandoned," then confiscated, properties to be reclaimed when the war ended, much less after a decade had elapsed.

Hannah had no one to advocate for her, and she was a young woman with no connections and no experience in such matters. Applying the lessons she learned so many years earlier—- self-reliance, perseverance, and a sense of fairness—once again served her well. I wondered how she was treated during this process.

It takes a lot of guts to deal with the German government. I was determined not to give up. I had some rights; I looked up those rights. It took several months to find out what my rights were as a survivor. My grandparents and parents were lost to me forever, and I wasn't about to give up my rights. I never had anybody to help me.

I sat on the steps of the government building for several months to force them to give me back some of my past. They said, 'No, we cannot, because we have those people in there.' I said, 'Well throw them out, because these houses are mine.' Every morning at seven o'clock I sat on the steps and waited for the clerk who worked with my stuff. Just after I was twenty-one, one morning I sat there and waited until she came. I put my claim in again, and she said, 'I think I can help you today.'

She showed me three pieces of land in Berlin that I could have for free. I just had to go look at them, and I could decide which one I wanted. So I got the most expensive land I ever owned in my life. It was in a very nice neighborhood on Lake Wannsee; that's why I picked it. It was not far from where my parents lived; I wanted to be near where my parents lived. There was green grass, and it was a little bit up on a hill. All around is water. But the water was parted (sic); half was Communist and half of it was in West Berlin. I took that land, and when I met my husband a year later, he built me a house on that land.

Wannsee is an affluent suburb of Berlin. It is noted historically for the conference held there January 20, 1942, organized by the infamous Reinhard Heydrich to formulate the "final solution" to the Jewish problem. Heydrich was later assassinated in Czechoslovakia. German retribution resulted in total destruction of the town-space and population of the village of Lidice.

At the time it was a widely publicized tragedy of the war. It is ironic that Hannah found such fulfillment in Wannsee.

In medical school Hannah learned some things about herself that surprised her.

The first two semesters were fine. I learned easily. Speech, reading, and writing were no problem. I was good in books, but in practice I was very bad, because when I saw blood I was down on the floor. We were assigned to the nursing staff in a hospital to do what the nurses do. But caring for patients made me sick. If someone threw up, I couldn't stay next to it. I couldn't stand to see blood, and I went out when we started to go into the morgue. There was no way I could continue.

Yes, it surprised me very much, because I wanted to get into medicine badly. This mystified me. If you asked me to do something, I could tell you if I learned it in a book. I was an 'A' student in the books, but practical was not my side. I couldn't get myself to stand in an operating room and watch an operation. Especially I couldn't stand to handle the cadavers in the morgue* and would pass out when we had to work on one. I don't know if it relates to my camp experience. To this day I can't stand to see blood. I can't stand to see an accident. If I were asked to help, I couldn't do that. I went to the Red Cross once to learn to revive someone, but I don't think I could do that either.

I love chemistry. I love biology and everything medicine has to do with—doing experiments on mice—everything,

---

*In American universities, what Hannah refers to as the morgue is the gross anatomy laboratory.

but as soon as it came to human beings and dissecting them, I couldn't do it. So I decided I had to do something besides medicine and just stay with chemistry, because I loved chemistry and I didn't want to give it up.

Hannah earned a Ph.D. in chemistry in 1965 from the University of Berlin. In the meantime, while at the university, Hannah was protesting against nuclear power.

I put myself in the position that I handcuffed myself to the power plant fence, that is, where they were going to build a power plant. I was arrested several times. I wasn't going to give up, until that day Rudi Dutsche got shot right in front of me. We were holding a rally. He was standing on a platform so everyone could see him, and he was talking into a loud speaker. Someone shot him in the head from not very far away with a shotgun. Rudi was also a medical student and one of the best. He is still alive, a professor in London. After that happened to Rudi, we gave up. We could see it wasn't going to change anything, and it wasn't worth getting shot.

Rudi's assailant was apprehended and sentenced to fifteen years. I think Hannah and her friends were learning first hand what Confuscious taught us many years ago, something to the effect that if your enemy has power over you, don't fight it.

Chapter Five

Other people should be important in our lives.
— Hannah

O n November 1ˢᵗ of 1960, not many months after Hannah's property settlement with the government, another major milestone was reached.

One day I stopped at a kiosk/snack bar type of structure where one could buy cigarettes, a newspaper, coffee, a beer. I was getting my newspaper and on my way home. I struck up a conversation with an American serviceman who was reading a paper and having a beer. I learned his name was Wayne, he was a second lieutenant stationed at Frankfurt, a flyer graduated from the Air Force Academy in Colorado Springs, Colorado.

He invited me to the PX for dinner that night; they had a restaurant there. It was Monday night steak night, and we ordered steak. I said, 'What is this?' Wayne explained. I had one piece of that steak, and I'm telling you from that day on I wanted steak every day! I LOVED it!

The second date we went out for dinner too, and I knew he was the right man for me. It took two or three dates before we even revealed to each other that we were Jewish. German people were just getting used to Jewish people again; it wasn't something you said right away. We were both shocked to find each other. I always thought God had a hand in my meeting my husband.

On the third date he asked me to marry him, but we had to hurry because he was being sent to Turkey on temporary duty at an air base there. I had to become an American citizen to marry him, since he had a security clearance. We went to his commander, who interviewed me and actually had the nerve to ask me if I had ever been a Nazi. I put my papers in, but the general said, 'I can't make you a citizen in thirteen days.' Wayne said, 'Yes, you can.' And it happened. I gave up my German citizenship and my Israeli citizenship. I didn't want to be a German citizen anymore. I could have kept my Israeli citizenship and have dual citizenship with America. I am entitled to, but I didn't want to. When I became an American citizen I became a patriotic American, and I still am. If America would ask me to fight for America, I would do so—for my husband and for my son. We were married in the synagogue and also at the German Standesamt. In Germany you have to have a civil and a church wedding.

At this point Hannah made a startling admission, startling because she has established herself as an extremely independent, self-reliant individual. But it isn't surprising that with her background, Hannah would long for the luxury of relief now and then from total responsibility.

I always wanted someone to take care of me, and Wayne was the only one who ever did that. I didn't have to do anything; my husband did it all. I knew I could depend on him to advocate for me.

Shortly after they were married, Wayne accompanied Hannah back to Dachau.

There was no museum, nothing else at that time. We just looked at the empty buildings and didn't go through. We didn't stay very long. There was nothing formal to designate the site. *

*Establishing a memorial site and museum did take time. Construction and improvements continued over several years, but "doors opened" in 1961 when the first exhibit was shown.

They weren't ready; it was too soon after the war. Remember, it took until 1953 for the Germans to build something up. They didn't have time or resources for such things. It took a long time. I think the first time I could say that Berlin was pretty much built up was about 1967 or '68. It was pretty much done then, but not completely.

This author was in Germany including Munich in 1951, and there was still much evidence of destruction in many German localities. At that time, there was no talk of and probably little interest in visiting sites of former concentration camps.

After that we went to see the nuns at the convent. We spent a day there. We ate there, stayed overnight, and we got everybody together. They were talking about me, what kind of a girl I was.

And no doubt they were pleased to see how well Hannah had done in the few years since she left the convent.

Yes, they were. And the funny part of it was, they spoke perfect English in addition to Hebrew, German, Latin, and classical Greek. It was a pleasure that my husband got to meet those nuns, because by that time they were pretty old. A lot of them had died.

At Christmastime Wayne and Hannah traveled to Iowa to meet Wayne's mother. He was an only child and had already lost his father to an accident when Wayne was twelve.

His mother wanted him to farm the family land, but Wayne had no interest in taking over the farm, although he liked to help with the crops when he was home.

In 1961 about the same time I gave up being a medical student and switched to chemistry, Wayne started to build our house on the Wannsee land I received from the government. The conversion rate was good for Wayne's American paycheck, and we were able to make substantial savings. Every cent we could spare went into supplies, lumber, bricks.

Each of us also had a second job. When Wayne wasn't flying, he became a teacher to teach other pilots. I took a job with a travel agency while I was going to the university. Every spare minute, and there weren't many, we worked on the house.

It took nearly three years to complete it, because Wayne was gone a lot and so was I. We were very proud of that house. It had nine bedrooms, because we wanted a large family—enough for our own soccer team! We moved in in 1963 just before our son Brian was born.

What was this man like, who had stolen the heart of our heroine? Was he like Hannah?

Not at all. Wayne was timid and shy. We were a good combination. But he had -- what do you call it when someone has the overhand (sic) over you? He was gentle but had a very dominant way.

I told her we call that "walking softly and carrying a big stick." She liked that.

He was a spokesman for me, and I shut up for once. We never had a fight. We didn't argue. I said my mind; he said his. We had a lot of respect for each other. We both understood that we had to do it that way.

Wayne had assignments in Pakistan, Turkey, and Anchorage, and Hannah with Brian sometimes went with him. In 1967,

Wayne was sent to Vietnam. Hannah remained in Germany and was still working at the travel agency. She could pick her times and where she wanted to go. Everywhere Hannah went, she took Brian, with a nanny—later with a tutor. She planned tours while Wayne was off on TDY (temporary duty of less than six months). He was usually gone for two months at a time.

On Christmas Eve of 1967, Wayne was reported missing in action in Vietnam after just two months of his tour of duty as a B52 pilot.

When the colonel came to the door and gave me the news, I didn't react much at all. I didn't believe him. I said 'Okay,' thanked him, and closed the door. Brian was four years old when this happened. I couldn't accept that Wayne was gone, and for ten years I kept hoping something would turn up.

Now completely on her own, Hannah set new goals and managed her own therapy. She began work on a doctorate in music, mastering the piano and harp and continuing the training and passion she first acquired at the convent. She completed that degree in 1972 from the University of Berlin.

Hannah had tickets for the Olympics in Munich in 1972. She wanted Brian to see this event that had been a part of her life for so many years. It was the second time Israel had sent teams to the games. When news came of the massacre of the Israeli team, Hannah and Brian were in their hotel in Munich.

When I heard about it, I took my car, I took my son, and off I went home from Munich all the way to Berlin. We had to go through the wall, and we were totally alone on that whole highway. That's how I hightailed it out of there, as fast as I could.

During the postwar era, I think it would be safe to say that non-Jewish Americans gave little thought to Jews being in danger outside of the Middle East, certainly not in Germany again. Hannah, however, has never been completely free, even in America, from looking over her shoulder. In Germany she didn't identify herself as being Jewish or a Holocaust survivor. She reports that the survivors she knew there behaved in the same way, not overtly threatened but existing in a state of uneasiness. Postwar attitudes as she experienced them will be discussed in a later chapter.

In 1977 the Pentagon organized a trip to Vietnam for wives of MIAs seeking information and some kind of closure.

The State Department wrote us saying there were still some American prisoners alive in Vietnam, and they might be in jail. I took Brian with me; he was fourteen. Two other women had their children with them. There were seven women in all. We had an American diplomat with us, because there were all American women.

First of all we stayed over in Hanoi and waited until they gave us cars and buses. They took us everywhere, down to Laos, stopping to look at jails, and into cities where they kept prisoners. We knew they wouldn't have shown us any American captives if they had them, and there was no one non-Vietnamese to ask. Nobody was expecting anything. We were there for four weeks and could not find a trace of any Americans living there. The trip was long and very emotional. It was an education for Brian.

After we came back to Germany, Brian and I went together to Dachau. By that time there was a museum with a big plaque with all the names. That was the last time I went there. After that I brought Brian to the convent where I grew up. I wanted to live there for a year or two and put Brian in the convent school, but he didn't want any part of it. I let him decide what he wanted to do about that.

These were interesting though difficult times to be living in Berlin. Fortunately Hannah and Brian lived in West Berlin.

At first you couldn't get out of the city except by train, later the lift via Pan Am. It was forty kilometers in each direction to get into West Germany from Berlin. It was a long and tedious process to pass through on land. Driving into the communist zone you're always scared they're going to catch you. You don't have to do anything for them to put you in jail, and you don't want to be very long in that 'dead zone.' You just drive as slow as you can, then as fast as you can to get out of there. You don't talk to anybody, you don't smile to anybody.

One time when I was driving an RV from Seattle to California, someone stopped me and asked if I had fruit. It reminded me of checkpoint Charlie; that was funny to me. I'm used to things like that, but I didn't expect it in California!

At the time of writing (2004), a Russian commercial airplane had just crashed, and terrorism was suspected as the cause. Reports claimed little or no security presently exists in Russian airports. This is quite unlike what travelers experienced during the Cold War.

Russians were a lot more security-conscious during the Cold War than they are today. That's why they maintained control for so long; they knew what security was all about, and they sure had effective security around Berlin. I lived in Berlin with the Wall. It was uncomfortable having the guards train their binoculars our way. Berliners lived like that for thirty-five years, but otherwise we lived well, in its shadow. One gets accustomed to what is.

When President Reagan came to Berlin and visited the wall in 1987, I went to see the American president. Among the crowd around the podium, I asked him to do what he could to get the wall torn down. He assured us that some day it would come down, and we all should do what we could to see that it happened. We never thought it would come down.

I was there that night with a hammer. The wall was difficult to bring down, and we never dreamed we could do that. The night it came down was a night of riotous celebration.

Hannah and Wayne, the only photo Hannah has of Wayne

The house built at Wannsee overlooking the lake. Note the line across the lake which Hannah described as where "the water was parted. . .," meaning the demarcation separating West Berlin from the Russian zone. The closest part is in West Berlin. The Wall, unseen here, ran along the right side of the lake.

WAYNE

Brian at 18

Chapter Six

BRIAN

In order to get along with people,
you have to have humility.
— Hannah

After Wayne was reported missing, Hannah devoted her energies to raising Brian and bringing him up in his father's image. Brian was only four years old when he lost his daddy.

We did our Christmas even though Wayne wasn't there. Then I went back to work and more work. For ten years I waited before I would declare Wayne dead. After that I never had another man in my life, and I didn't even consider that an option. For me, my responsibility was to get this child grown up and to be like his dad. Sometimes I think it was wrong, but that was the only thing I knew. There was nothing I wouldn't have done for Brian. I thought if I make him as smart as Wayne, and if he has a little bit of me, he'll get along in life very well. I did a good job, because he was just like Wayne. But he didn't remember his dad because he was so young.

From a child on, I raised him to be a man, to be responsible for himself and for me. He learned to cook and bake and would have dinner ready when I came home from work. He was always an 'A' student, and I never had to worry about him in school.

During those years without Wayne, Hannah traveled internationally. She became the director of the travel agency, an association she maintained for over thirty years. While Brian was young, he accompanied her everywhere.

After Wayne died, my first world cruise was on the QE2. I took Brian with me, along with a tutor. We sailed around the world, my first big tour. After this I did world cruises every year; sometimes I flew tours, to Australia, New Zealand, South America, Galapagos, Samoa, Easter

Island, Tahiti, Singapore, Hong Kong, China, India, Pakistan, Saudi Arabia, Kuwait, Russia, Kenya—the whole world.

When Brian was sixteen he decided he wanted to learn to be a pilot and be like his dad. We flew to my mother-in-law's home in Sand Point, Idaho at the time, to have him learn to fly. We did this for a few summers. It gave Brian a chance to know his grandmother, his only relative.

Hannah's relationship with Wayne's mother was less than satisfying, especially for someone who longed to expand her personal, familial circle.

We never quarreled, but I felt like she didn't like me. She blamed me for his staying in the Air Force. I had nothing to do with that, of course. He went to the Air Force Academy in Colorado Springs. He had to have approval from the governor of Iowa in order to do that. He was four years in the academy, and he was required to do eight more years in the US Air Force. He was sent to Germany, and I met him there, so there was nothing that had anything to do with me.

Perhaps Wayne's mother was trying to rationalize Wayne's tragic fate and place blame on her only reachable target.

Brian didn't find her to be a typical grandmother. They didn't seem to warm to each other. But I thought it was important for Brian to be familiar with his half-American roots, and so we came regularly to visit her.

The sad and unfair conclusion to this episode came when Wayne's mother died intestate. She had been urged for a long time to make a will, but she refused to do so, fearful of the prospect of death. As a result, her farm and other property went to the state instead of to Brian. Hannah feels that this exclusion was deliberate, pointed directly at her and prompted by Wayne's mother's fear that her estate would fall into Hannah's hands. *"She hurt him to get at me."* In reality, it was Brian who lost—resources he could have applied to his advanced education, to starting a business, or to give economic security to both of them. Hannah's loss was the sting of final rejection by someone whose approval she sought. Wayne's mother in return made it clear by this gesture that she never had accepted or trusted Hannah.

When Brian was eighteen, he declared he wanted to become an astronaut. We made inquiries at NASA, then flew to Florida intending to enroll Brian at Florida State University in Tallahassee. NASA had a separate training program in Tallahassee for astronauts, but Brian had bad eyes, which disqualified him for that program. Instead, he entered a NASA course of study that focused on computer technology.

He moved into an apartment in Tallahassee, and I lived with him for a month. Every two weeks after that I flew to Florida to see him. During the day he went to school; at night he made pizzas. Finally he said to me, 'Mom, you've got to let me go.' That was the hardest time for me, to let Brian go.

Brian later earned a doctorate in computer software from DeVry University in Phoenix. This degree had a medical component to it, which equipped him for some of the work he later did for NASA in San Diego, responsibilities that included, for example, the measurement of blood pressure of astronauts in space.

Chapter Seven

LA VIE INTERNATIONALE

To have friends takes a lot of work.
You have to work at friendship every day.
— Hannah

Despite the heartbreak of Wayne's disappearance and later seeing Brian go off on his own to America, Hannah lived a full and productive life as an American citizen in Berlin, until 1993 when her world would turn upside down once again.

She had maintained a serious interest in music, nurtured and cultivated throughout her years at the convent. After completing her academic work in chemistry, she continued to increase her mastery of the piano and harp by returning to the university for academic accreditation in music. She obtained a part-time position performing with the Berlin Symphony under the direction of Prof. Dr. Rolf Weiss. Hannah maintained that relationship for seven years, working in rehearsals and concert performances between tour obligations abroad. Her doctorate in music from the University of Berlin was earned all the while she continued her affiliation with the travel agency.

Traveling always yields stories worth repeating, and Hannah's multiple years in the industry are no exception. As a professional, her experiences seem more numerous, more unique, and often more hair-raising than the ordinary traveler encounters, as she made twenty-five trips around the world. She could get your attention with comments like *"Did I tell you about the TWA flight to New York when we got hi-jacked, and they threw the pilot out the window?*

I don't remember what year it was in the 1980s. Perhaps you read about it in the newspapers. My company was planning a cruise to New York. I was going ahead of time, because we didn't have it completely booked, and I was trying to find more tourists to book from that end. About three or four hours out of New York, approaching New York, five or six men took over. They showed us hand grenades and guns, ordered us around, and there was a lot of shouting and screaming. They were Palestinians sent by Arafat. They wanted Palestinian leaders to be let out of jail, and so they were looking for Israelis. They looked at everybody's passport and knew where everybody came from. Thank God I had an American passport.

As soon as someone shouted, 'Duck!' I ducked and went down on the floor and didn't come up. I didn't want to see them or be able to identify them. There were people who got shot. I thought this was my end and there wasn't anything I could do, so I just laid there like I was dead. After we landed, the pilot wouldn't do what they were demanding that he do—I don't know what it was—they threw the pilot out of the cockpit window. That's very high up in those big planes, and he was killed by the fall. It was a long time before we were freed. Finally some kind of military or police riot squad or something like that freed us, but that was the scariest thing of my life.

Another time I had a Lufthansa flight out of New York, and we had a hole blown into the plane from a lightning strike over the ocean. We had just left New York, out about an hour and a half going to Frankfurt, when lightning struck and we got a big hole in the back. We all had to put those masks on for a while. Then we dropped in altitude and flew on to Frankfurt 3000 feet high. When you saw those waves on the ocean so close, you just thought you were going down any minute.

Then there was the time we had a boat trip from Los Angeles to Alaska, maybe fifteen or twenty years ago. A 78-year-old woman had her lover with her. He was 35 or

40 years old. She was stabbed to death in her cabin. We had to stop in Seattle to get the lady's body off, and we had to stay there for two days because they had to find the murderer. My group got very nervous about that. It was the lover who did it, and they found him. Then we could go on to Alaska.

In the late 1970s, we were on a world cruise on the QE2 for three months. A 70-year old lady died on the tour from a heart attack. When this happens, the tour operator has to go with the body in order to arrange to fly it home on another flight, in this case from Noreeta Airport in Tokyo. We had taken refuge in Tokyo Bay from a typhoon. The ship had already been anchored there for three days. There wasn't an icebox to put the lady's body in, and we couldn't leave it on the boat because it was decomposing. Because of the typhoon, a helicopter had to come and pick up the body and me to fly to the airport to get her onto a plane back to Germany. I had to accompany the body to the airport. There was just the body, the pilot, and me. I don't like to fly anyway, and I was never so scared in my life riding in a helicopter in that storm. We went to the airport in such a typhoon you wouldn't believe. When we landed, we tipped over sideways like this, and I thought my life was done.

There was another problem at the airport when we were ready to ship the casket home. We found out she didn't have her birth certificate with her. I always told my clients to bring along a birth certificate and driver's license as well as their passport, in case of emergency, but this lady apparently didn't do that. They wouldn't let me ship her back to Germany. I had to contact her relatives in Germany so they could pick her up in Tokyo. I needed to get back to the ship, but they wouldn't let me leave the casket. I had to wait there until a relative came from Germany to claim the body. The boat had to wait for me for five more days.

I had a tour to Rome several years ago, which included a tour of the Vatican. In the convent we learned about Pope Pius XII. The nuns gave out pictures, including one of Pius XII. We met with Pope John 23rd during our tour, and I had this picture of Pius XII with me. We got a medal from the pope because of our tour there. I didn't say it very loud to him, but I did tell him I was saddened when I came out of the Holocaust that Pius XII didn't honor more our Jews. He said to me, 'I don't know how you survived, but I think you should write this down and write a book what you remember and then send us one.' And that's all he said. No, it wasn't quite enough, but I understood what he meant, because he couldn't criticize in front of all those people. He gave me a smile and said what he said. At that time, the Vatican didn't approve the state of Israel yet. That came later, so he couldn't say much about the Jewish people at that time.

When I went to Kenya, on my birthday the Minister of Travel gave a birthday party for me. That was an odd thing, but I was very honored to have that, that he thought enough of me as travel director of a big corporation to do that to thank me.

There was another time in Kenya we got locked into our hotel because two tribes were fighting each other. We watched from our windows, scared to death they would come after us. They were at each other with spears!

Author had a very un-five-star experience in Kenya while on a solo to discover Africa. For my benefit, Masai friends were visiting relatives out in the bush not far from Nairobi. Received hospitably in three different bomas (native huts), at each we were served a mug of warm, sweet milk. Because it was sweet, and actually quite tasty, I inquired about it and was told simply that it was cow's milk. Later I learned its sweetness came from cow urine mixed in with the milk.

In Thailand near Bangkok in Xian, the prince and princess invited us for a tour of their palace, and we stayed there for three days. They opened up their palace for tourists in order to make money. It was in the tour package; we could eat and sleep there, etc., and we paid plenty for the privilege. They only did that for three or four years. The princess herself showed us around, and we were invited to see an elephant roundup. It's a big thing they do every year; in November they do this. These are trained, working elephants, and they bring them together from all around for a festival; they have a party for them.

Before the giant tsunami devastated the area in early January of 2005, most of us had never heard of Phuqet. In an earlier interview Hannah described Phuqet as another interesting, resort-type destination to visit in Thailand, "*. . .where the sand is clean and fine like in Florida, but the sand is black.*" After that recent disaster, Hannah's response was not what you were hearing in local coffee shops. "*I have been there many times over Christmas. When this happened I said, 'Thank you God, that I wasn't there this time.'*"

Excursions to Israel were also part of Hannah's routine. She

has already described how she wasn't received as a compa-
triot at that point, even though she was Jewish and had lived in
Israel. My natural response was, "What kind of a German wants
to go to Israel as a tourist?"

*Not many. My clients were mostly Swiss, Dutch, and
Luxembourgers, and their quest was more in the nature of
a Christian pilgrimage. I also took German Mormons to
see Salt Lake City.*

Hannah lived in China for two months in 1972 when she
opened an office for Royal Viking Line. In the process of several tours and business trips through the years, she added Canton
Chinese to her list of linguistic accomplishments—an asset to
someone doing frequent international travel.

*Before Mao there were German schools in China. Many
Chinese speak German rather than English. I don't like
China much; it is too past-oriented. They live in the past
instead of the future. They do have it better today than
they did before 1989; it isn't so regimented now. They
used to have to wear the same clothes, like uniforms.
Poverty is everywhere.*

*I wasn't comfortable with the poverty in China, or India,
Mexico and such places. When you see the way children
go to school. . . the old people that come to beg for food
at the hotels and hospitals, it reminds me of being behind
barbed wire holding out a hand for a piece of bread.
That's not living; it's just surviving. There are so many
bad stories from China; they are even worse than mine.*

In contrast to the deprivations of life in China . . .

I lived for four weeks in the Beverly Wilshire Hotel on

Rodeo Drive in Hollywood, because I had clients who wanted to make a shopping trip there. I used to have tours two or three times a year for people who wanted to shop. Americans do that to Paris or Italy or London, even New York. My people would go home after a week, and other people would come for the next week, etc. We would see movie stars everywhere. They didn't mean anything to me, but my guests would get excited to go to the pool and see someone they would recognize. This hotel is where they made the movie "Pretty Woman." I was in one of those suites where they were. For four weeks that was quite a treat. I had my office up there. They even gave me my own butler.

Nevertheless, such luxury was quite out of Hannah's character to appreciate or enjoy. Five-course meals bored her, as well as the cuisine, which was often not palatable to her tastes. When on tour she preferred to have simple food served in her room or on the balcony while she looked at the view and did her work. Gourmet meals were not of interest to her either, not to mention being aware of how much weight one could gain being exposed regularly to such opportunities for gluttony. On cruises, eating at the captain's table was de rigueur, in a long dress—a privilege for which people paid heavily but which was not relished by Hannah.

Then she made some surprising confessions about this glamorous life "on the road."

I looked forward to getting where we were supposed to go so I could get rid of the water under me! Cruises were always a stress for me, because I can't swim. I won't go up in the Eiffel Tower in Paris because it's too high. I am not comfortable flying either. It's a survival thing. But I had to go on cruises and fly in airplanes because that was my work, and I was always scared to get on a boat and scared to get on an airplane. Nobody saw how I was holding up that airplane with my hands!

The original white-knuckle passenger, she readily admits. Determined as she is to maneuver herself headlong through whatever she must do, she resolved to get over her fear of flying. *"I tried the champagne served in first class, but that didn't do it. It only made me sick. I never got over it."*

Regarding the comparative safety of air travel opposed to driving on the interstate to Denver, Hannah observed that it was the lack-of-control issue in the air that she couldn't reconcile. Given Hannah's keen sense of independence, her attitude is quite understandable, reasonable, and no doubt shared by other reluctant flyers. At the same time, many motorists on that stretch of I-25 have the same (justifiable) apprehensions. Hannah loved to travel, however, because she wanted to see the world, which is why she chose to go into the travel business.

At the beginning, I thought the world was flat. The nuns taught me the world is not flat. When I learned the world is round, that was the point for me to investigate why is the world round? So I got myself into learning about the earth, the stars, the moon, and the sun. I had to explain to myself what is going on if you travel from A to B to C—if I'm still floating or walking.

World travel provided a good livelihood for Hannah after Wayne's death. On the other hand, the luxurious life style that accompanied it was considered just a marginal bonus by Hannah. Simple joys bring meaning to her life, and she is thankful for that perspective despite the way it was forced upon her. It is ironic that she maintained those values amidst such luxury and among people whose reality and life expectations were so different from her own.

It wasn't me, nor were some of the people I served. Yes, there were prima donnas, those who would put a wad of bills wrapped in a rubber band into my hand and ask to be first or have the best suite. These tours were expensive, and many clients were very wealthy people. There were always some who expected to receive special treatment. Some people booked regularly, and they came to understand there was no favoritism on my tours. Everybody was treated the same, no matter who they were. Everybody thinks they are special, and they are. But keep it to yourself; you shouldn't expect other people to see you as special.

I let them know at the beginning I was in charge, and there were rules. There is just this much luggage, of these specifications. You will need your passport, birth certificate, and ID. This is the way it goes, and if you understand these things we will get along fine. If you don't, and if you make trouble on my tour, I'll refund your ticket and you can go home. I did it. I sent one home occasionally.

In the end, however, not every traveler has encountered as many famous or important world personages as Hannah did during her role leading international tours. Her list includes one pope, a Thai princess, a Kenyan government minister, and King Carlos of Spain while he was in exile in Holland. During her life in Germany as an ordinary citizen she was able to see two American presidents on their historic visits to Berlin. Besides meeting Ronald Reagan at the Wall, she was present in the crowd when JFK made his pronouncement "Ich bin ein Berliner." As an Olympic skier she counted Rosie Mittemeier,

Toni Sailer, and Waltraud Haas as friends—Olympic medal winners in the 1950s. Sailer was a gold medalist from Austria who won downhill in 1956. *"He bought a restaurant in Zell am See in Austria and we used to go to see him."*

The plum for name-dropping is her friendship with Queen Beatrix of Holland. Beatrix was sent to the convent when she was 18 years old to experience the "common" life for one year. I sneered, "Of course she didn't live in an ordinary dormitory room with four or five other people."

Hannah countered, *"You betcha she did. I saw her again soon after she married Prince Klaus. Klaus was very sick for many years; he just died. He had severe emotional problems, and it changed Beatrix a lot. She got so serious. When I knew her at the convent, she was a fun young girl, joking a lot. I saw her again after I got married; she invited Wayne and me for coffee. I saw her one more time when we had a tour in Holland, and I called her. She was just a friend I knew when I was young; I never thought of her as a queen."*

Ordinarily your tour director doesn't sidetrack in order to make a personal phone call to the queen?

Chapter Eight

TO AMERICA

We're never completely alone.
    –Hannah

Meanwhile, Brian was a computer scientist working for NASA and General Dynamics in San Diego. He was engaged to a German girl. Hannah was looking forward to his added fulfillment as a husband and father and the possibility of bringing grandchildren into her life.

Brian called me every day, wherever I was traveling in the world. On the seventh of March, 1993, I was at a hotel in Zurich with a tour. No call came. At one o'clock in the morning when the phone rang, I hoped it was Brian, but it was a morgue in San Bernardino, California, telling me that my son had died. He was piloting a rented civilian plane from San Diego to Big Bear Lake in San Bernardino County, with four adults and two children aboard. The plane couldn't take off properly, and it hit a house. Brian and an adult friend were the only fatalities. A year later the FAA determined that the plane hadn't been serviced right.

Hannah came to California for the funeral arrangements, deciding to bury Brian in western Idaho where Wayne's mother had last resided. It was the only American connection Hannah had left, and it was for Wayne's sake that she kept Brian in America. Of course Wayne had no known burial site. When it came time to return to Europe, Hannah psychologically couldn't leave. Half a dozen times she made arrangements to do so, but each time she could only get so far in the preparations and couldn't bring herself to go.

I don't want the memories of my husband and my son overseas. I couldn't live with that; that's why I stayed here. It's an accident that I'm here; I just never could go home. I called those people at the travel office and said I'm not coming back. I'm homesick sometimes for Germany, and sometimes I wish I never came. Not very often. This is my home now. It's my country. I'm an American, and I became an American for my husband. If I had known then when I was 22 how good life is here, I would have come at that time.

Hannah resettled in an apartment in eastern Washington state, because it was near Brian's burial site. Then she went into a long and dangerous seclusion. After the initial grief and activity associated with the tragedy, she apparently experienced some sort of shock. For several months she sat in her apartment staring into space, doing nothing, eating little. No help or even the barest attention was received from other tenants in the building, because Hannah wasn't visible and had never gotten acquainted with her neighbors. Her health deteriorated, and her mental condition was precarious.

Then one day an old lady with a little girl came to my door asking for food. I had no food but gave them a jar of coins.

She suddenly became aware of her own desperate situation and summoned help. A neighbor called 911, and Hannah was taken to a local hospital weighing 89 pounds. Two weeks later she was released and began looking for a job.

Hannah recognizes that her reaction to Brian's death was more severe than the way she responded to losing Wayne. The mother/son relationship between them was very strong, because Brian was all she had left after Wayne's disappearance. Brian's death was so completely unexpected, while Wayne was involved in a combat environment. After Wayne was reported missing, she had several years to adjust to the possibility he might not return, but the loss of Brian was final as announced.

When Brian died, I put it onto myself that I should never have allowed him to fly. Wayne was raised by his mom, who wanted him to be a farmer, but the only thing he wanted was to be a flyer. I don't think anybody else in his family flew. I just passed that on to Brian the best way I knew how, and he just took it away, what he wanted to be. It took a long time until I could finally say to myself, no, it wasn't my fault. We don't have that much control over other people. I had to turn back and realize he did what he loved, and he died doing that.

Losing my son was the worst thing that ever happened to me. I would go ten years in Dachau if I could have Brian back. That was the love of my life. My husband was the other, but I was with Wayne only seven years. There is a difference. It is a bonding sort of thing between a mother and child. When Wayne was missing, although Brian was only four years old he was there for me to hold on to. I sometimes thought if he were even in a wheelchair I could take care of him, but that was selfish of me. I don't think he would have liked that, but I would have enjoyed just having him with me.

No matter how old the lost child is, you never get over it. I still wait for Brian to call, especially at holidays like Christmas and Easter. When the phone rings I get a big butterfly in my stomach, and I think it's him. And it will never leave me. I go through it every day, when I get up, when I go down, and then I realize he isn't going to call. But it doesn't make me sad any more. It was something I had to work out myself.

Consistent with what she has already told us about learning

not to cry in the camp and not being able to cry throughout the rest of her life, Hannah was not able to cry over the deaths of Wayne and Brian. Her grief, however, had no boundary. Once more and most finally, there was no one to hold on to anymore. Hannah was assured of one thing; her heart could not be broken again.

Hannah and Wayne were happily married for seven years. Brian was twenty-nine when he was killed. His fiancée has never married.

Once Hannah realized she would not return to Europe, there was a matter of disposing of the house she and Wayne had built in Berlin. So distraught was she at the time, her resolution was dramatic and as simple and painless as possible. She gave the house and its furnishings to Berlin friends, a young couple who were close friends of hers and Wayne's, and they lived in a rented house in Berlin.

I didn't want the memories of it, and I didn't have any use for it anymore. I couldn't bring myself to sell it to strangers.

Then another bizarre turn of events shook up Hannah's progress in adjusting to a new life in America. At Christmastime in 1994, the recipients of the Berlin house went on a skiing trip and were killed when their car went off the road and down a mountainside.

So the German government gave the house back to me. That's the way it works overseas because I gave it to them without a purchase. They did not have children, and the law says they have to give it back to me. So I had to deal with this again. It took a while to get rid of it. I didn't have other friends to give it to; charity was out of the question. Except for the nuns there was no charity involved in my life, and for me, giving to charity there has to be a connection. It was not for the nuns anyway, because they were all old and lived far away from Berlin. They didn't have that convent any more. The house was sold eventually, and I didn't even want to know their name. I had a lawyer arrange to give the rest to Mother Teresa.

Needing to sustain herself by new employment, Hannah took a secretarial position in Washington state in a state-run social services agency catering to the domestic needs of senior citizens. Despite her impressive academic credentials, she lacked experience in those chosen fields and was embarking on a new career at mid-life in a foreign environment. She had found that the travel business in the U.S. was not the professional occupation it was in Europe, and in the U.S. it did not pay as well.

She remained in Washington for six years, then came to Colorado seeking a different locale in order to get away from the unpleasant associations with her mother-in-law. Responding to an advertisement for a job in Boulder, Hannah checked in at a motel in a nearby community. The position in Boulder didn't materialize, but the manager of the motel invited Hannah to stay on as staff. She became manager a short time later.

I think this is where I'm supposed to be. Was I meant to be alone? I'm not really alone. We're never completely alone.

After relocating in Colorado, Hannah brought Brian's remains from Idaho and re-interred them in a local cemetery. Hannah was the only person present at the ceremony.

Das Leben (The Life)
Nicht was wir erleben
sondern wie wir empfinden
Was wir erleben
Macht unser Schickral aus

Glücklich (Happy)
Halte das Glück wie ein Vogel
So leise und lose wie möglich
Dünkt er sich selber nur frei
ßleibt er dir gern in der Hand

-Hannah

Courtesy of Russian Film and Video Archive

PART II
Chapter Nine

Welcome criticism. If someone thinks enough of
me to tell me what's wrong, I want to know that.
— Hannah

I t is natural after absorbing Hannah's story and meeting her as a warm, mature adult, to want to know how or if the camp experience has impacted the succeeding years. Some survivors are bitter, while others feel blessed just to be alive. Some fight with guilt for their selected survival, while others are bewildered by it. Some are eager to share—to inform and educate the public—while others choose to be silent. Hannah has never been exposed to counseling or analysis, and it is not my mission to present her as a psychological case study. Her own words reveal someone who knows what she is, who she is (within a somewhat narrower definition of that concept), and why she is. She is a proud, confident, yet modest individual, displaying an infectious sparkle that belies the roller coaster life she has led.

It is important to remember that traumatic and unnatural as those formulating years were for Hannah, her development as a human being did not begin or end with liberation in 1945. For all of us, whatever goals we reach, whatever loss and disappointments are inflicted upon us or we bring onto ourselves, life goes on. Time is an impossible force to stop. Winning the Super Bowl isn't the end. Losing an election isn't the end. Surviving serious illness isn't the end. And certainly getting the kids through college isn't the end. Like the rest of us, Hannah has a lifetime accumulation of experiences, responses to stimuli, relationships, and all that bring us to where we are—for the moment.

A primary issue to consider is her health. Can the long-term effects be determined of: deprived diet and lack of protein and calcium, lack of dental hygiene and professional care, unknown medical experiments, prolonged exposure to the elements, and lack of basic sanitary practices. Are they manifest? Hannah appears robust and healthy but has some serious health issues. Are genetics involved?

The physical brutality in the camps is beyond words to describe. That the human body can survive so many assaults on its structure and function is hard to explain. Several years ago while visiting the healing shrine at Lourdes in France, I asked a physician who was present about the crutches on the wall and wheelchairs left behind by supposedly "cured" pilgrims. He said there are instances that defy medical justification; they appear to have no other explanation than miracle. We all know of individuals who have made inexplicable recoveries of one kind or another, and science is left speechless. My own husband had a history-making case of spinal meningitis seventy years ago when he was nine years old. His spinal count was so high the specialist consulted in another city wouldn't even bother to attend him. It was before antibiotics were developed, and the family was told to make funeral arrangements. His count continued to elevate until it was so far off the charts no one could believe what was happening. Seventy-nine at this writing, his only long-term effect is hearing loss in one ear. Should we discount faith, will, and prayer in these unexplained cases?

In the camps, thousands of victims were regularly exposed to the harshest extremes of the elements, daily and for long periods of time, without footwear, clad only in cotton pajama-type uniforms. They stood barefoot for hours in the cold and snow, even forced to walk long distances under those same conditions. As a hardship, living in unheated barracks pales in comparison; at least enclosure provided shelter from the wind and blowing snow and opportunities for bodies to warm each other.

What particularly puzzles me is this: in Colorado where outdoor winter activity is popular, hikers, hunters, and skiers are cautioned about the dangers of being caught unprepared in capricious mountain weather. On a single occasion, hypothermia can easily overtake an inadequately dressed sportsman, with possibly serious consequences. We careful mothers are convinced that if our children aren't properly capped and mittened on their way to school, they will surely become ill. President William Henry Harrison, at his inauguration in 1841, supposedly got over-chilled during frigid outdoor ceremonies, contracted pneumonia and died a month later. Is that a scientific diagnosis of cause and effect?

While many camp internees did succumb to frostbite and death, thousands did not. Only one physician I consulted had a suggestion—that perhaps acclimatizing or self-regulation had occurred. Eskimos can obviously handle colder temperatures than a Caribbean islander can. A holiday skier from Miami is at greater risk than the crew that daily grooms the slopes. Hardships in the camps were so extreme, so extended in time, not to mention in combination with other weakening forces, it seems there would be a limit beyond which an organism could not accommodate

I used to go to Finland to ski cross-country. I would go outside in the snow in my bathing suit, then go to the sauna. It didn't bother me a bit. I think I could still do that. I always wondered why my feet and my nose and ears didn't freeze in the camp, but that was different.

Hannah did not leave her miracles behind at Dachau.

In 1984 I was planning to go to Hawaii to do a triathlon; I was a runner, biker, and swimmer. For that I needed a doctor's certificate to travel to Honolulu to participate. The doctor found these lumps and said I had cancer. He

*put me in the hospital that day, and I didn't come out
for six months. I had chemo, lost my hair twice, some of
my stomach was removed, and I had several surgeries because of cancer. They didn't give me more than a year to
live, and I'm still here. I was in the hospital until I had
enough, and I just walked out. I said that's it; I don't care
if I die tomorrow, I'm getting out of this hospital. That
was in Berlin. Three months later I was back to running,
and I went back to work at my old job.*

She had heart surgery in 2003 and has stents inserted into
her heart. Macular degeneration, substantial hearing loss, even
recurrence of malaria contracted in Kenya are additional conditions she manages. She still jogs daily and skis whenever she
can. And no matter what is ailing her, she reports to work at the
motel.

Hannah's psychological recovery is equally remarkable.
The residue manifests itself in peculiar ways, but we all have
quirks, and hers may or may not be the result of experiences in
the camp.

*I am most comfortable in the dark with a little light on. I
grew up in the camp with cold and darkness. I am afraid
of the dark, always sleep with a light on, and the TV with
the sound turned off runs all night. I can't go into a dark
place like a garage or an attic. I wouldn't jog at night
without someone to go with me. At the same time, I don't
like bright sun either—one thing I didn't like about Israel.
I just like subdued light. And I don't bear heat well.*

We discussed how people react in extreme opposition to
negative stimuli. For example, an alcoholic's offspring are
sometimes alcoholic or abstaining. An abused child sometimes

becomes an abuser or is solicitous and gentle with children. Survivor attitudes toward food provide other relevant illustrations. Some of Hannah's friends from internment acquired food compulsions. Hannah, on the other hand, is indifferent to food. She eats once a day; her tastes are easily satisfied, and she doesn't have a good appetite.

I can't eat a lot. I never get hungry or even think about eating. I talked to people in Israel about that. Some people would eat so much, then wake up in the night and eat some more. Maybe they were afraid they wouldn't get any more to eat again. I don't drink water at all except mineral water without flavor. That's a European thing anyway; there it's coffee and wine. I don't go out to eat, even to be sociable.

What I do is buy things and store them. I store cans of food, like spaghetti. If there were an emergency and I couldn't get out to buy food, I have enough stored to feed ten people for six months! I keep candles and flares; I have a stove and bags you can crawl in to keep warm. I also have that sort of thing at all times in my car. I have an emergency kit that I put together and I am never without it: bandages, eye drops, everything you could possibly think of in case I get some place and can't get back.

It is not unusual for some Coloradoans to employ a similar strategy to be prepared for emergencies on the road, particularly in winter because of the state's unpredictable and sometimes violent weather.

I don't do it because of the weather; it's in case something goes wrong in the world, and I can't go where I want to go. I also have an emergency plan in case of something like a bomb attack, and I know which way and which route I go to get out of here. I keep the gas tank filled. I'm terrified of the police; they remind me of guards with their guns, and sirens sound like bombs falling.

These preferences and prejudices are minor. Hannah is otherwise consistently positive and in control. Some of her camp companions did not fare so well. Through the years some have committed suicide, including four close male friends.

I had a friend I always kept in contact with. We left on the same flight for Israel. We were in the same army, and he stayed there when I left. He was practically my best friend, three years older than me, and we always talked. He had a very hard time, worse than I did. I was there when he got married and was at his home a lot. He later became a physician in Bat Yam in Israel.

His wife called in November of 2003 to tell me he had died from an overdose. He left a note saying, 'I cannot live with the earlier years. I'm sorry, but I can't deal with this any more.' He tried all his life. He tried to tell a certain amount to his children—he had nine of them. I can't understand why he would do that, and I will never forgive him. After all the things we went through, why would you take your life and leave nine children and a wife behind you? That's not fair to anybody. He was a good physician, successful, prosperous, and had a good income. But he was a tormented individual, who had it worse than me because he was older than me.

It was always harder on the older kids, because they remembered their parents. Sometimes I have a hard time liv-

ing too, but it's just for a split second. It's not like I ponder on it all the time.

The forty kids that were alive after we had all left the convent stuck together, always tried to keep in touch with each other. I had a small black book with everybody's name and address in it. We tried to get together every five years. Most went to Israel, to England, and to the States. Those three places we were always able to stay in contact with each other. Not often, mostly for Hanukkah. Everybody wrote, and then you could find out who died. We kept track among ourselves; we didn't have anything like a 'class secretary.'

With regular emotional support in her present situation coming from just a few close friends, Hannah's outlook, at least what she presents to the public, is positive and upbeat.

I never went to a psychologist, because I don't believe in headshrinkers (sic). People say they would probably go a lot deeper, but nobody would get anything out of me if I didn't want them to. I say I don't need anybody to tell me that I have forgotten what I went through, that I didn't realize it. I know what I remember; that's what I give out. If there is something forgotten in that life, nobody needs to know. In order to go through this with a shrink, I don't want to and I don't need to.

The emotional stability of a three-year-old is so fragile, we both expressed our failure to comprehend how the younger children at the camp could tolerate the fear-filled environment in which they existed. Hannah's conjecture, based on her own experience:

First of all, you learn from the beginning—and I don't

know how I learned it—my instinct must have said every time somebody gonna cry, that guy is going to take his shiny thing and . . . what did I know about a gun? How did I learn this? I didn't have anybody to teach me. Something in me said, 'There's something wrong here.' That first day I probably started to cry. I don't know if I did or not. But I never cried again after I learned that lesson. The older I got, the more I just thought it was the right decision that I do this or that.

I raised myself until I was eight, then somebody else came in and raised me. At the convent I listened and I did, and I listened and I did. I would do anything for those nuns. Sometimes I was a little rebellious, tho. I remember I seemed to be the only one who always got caught for everything. I don't know why; maybe it was because I wouldn't lie. I couldn't lie. I got a red face if somebody would just look at me. I got scared and stopped doing whatever I was doing wrong. That's how I raised Brian, and that's probably where it came from. I never raised my voice to him. I never raised my hand. He tried, but with me he didn't get anywhere. He just needed to look into my eyes, and he knew that was not what he was supposed to do.

You can do that to me still today! If I would say something and it wouldn't be true, I couldn't answer you. I was in the doctor's office the other day for some trouble with my ear, and I was asked, 'How many do you smoke?' I couldn't say yes and I couldn't say no, and I got a red face, and the doctor said, 'I know how many you smoke!' Naturally she scolded me. I started to smoke when Brian died. I will

105

probably stop when I'm lying in the hospital with another something wrong with my heart.

I added my own bit of scolding—smoking with stents in your heart yet!

I don't trust just anybody. It takes a long time for me to become a trusting person. I am very careful selecting my friends, and I don't trust anybody fully. I always have it in the back of my mind the doubt that somebody wants to hurt me.

Having lost so much, it's a justifiable fear that something will be taken away from her.

When I entered Hannah's life as a complete stranger, she had every reason to question my motives, my honesty, as well as my competence in recording and interpreting her life. For my part, I couldn't help feeling regret that in order to accomplish our goal—to give voice to those 145 silent children— she had to spend hour upon hour reliving many unpleasant, best-forgotten experiences. This she did generously, honestly, and gracefully.

It was the length of time it took to pull this project together that benefited the book itself. Time produced gradual revelations and sharing of her intimate thoughts, her philosophical conclusions about herself and life in general. The Holocaust memoirs I have read don't go into such detail about the aftermath of their experience, but therein lies the lessons. I was proud to earn her confidence, as uncomfortable as some sessions were to hear and to write about. For her willingness to share those details, she is to be commended.

I never wanted to talk about it before. When Brian died,

that's when I became a talker. I have no idea why it came out, and I do feel better talking about it.

Hannah's musical expertise is regrettably a thing of the past, although she remains a lover and patron of good music.

I don't play any more, like a lot of things since Brian died. I don't have a piano and have lost interest. For whom would I play? There is no one to share it with, and I don't need to do it any more. I run, walk, ski, and work. I read a lot, not novels but something I can learn from.

What does she read? Her answer startled me—chemistry books! A monologue, not dialogue, followed that I can't repeat because I didn't understand it, and the tape recorder sputtered and hissed from the strain. *"People think I'm nuts."* No comment. *"I want to learn about modern chemistry to keep up with what's going on today, especially how it relates to advances in medicine."*

Hannah has a strong social conscience and well-defined morality. I asked her how, without guidance or role models, she developed this understanding of the difference between right and wrong and the importance of making the moral choice. She didn't have a ready answer for that, although she has obviously thought about it.

I believe in the rule of law, that people should obey the laws, not harm anyone, and be truthful. I really don't know where I got this. I too wonder why. It didn't come from the nuns. I did it myself. I decided I would go by the law. I knew I had to go by the rules until I was 18. The nuns had rules, and I just took over from them because I didn't know any better. After so long, you figure it out yourself.

Then I made my own rules. The rule I had then was 'don't get pregnant before you get married.' I figured that out because I would see someone with a baby and wasn't married, and I certainly didn't want to be in that position. Because of the sexual abuse at the camp, I didn't want to be doing that anyway. I think that had everything to do with it. I told myself if you find a man that you love, after you get married that's what you can do. I had men friends. I was in a kibbutz and had friends there. But I was the only one who didn't do what everybody else was doing. I was an outsider and a loner in that way. In another way I made jokes and laughed and had fun.

Earlier we discussed Hannah's failure to be impressed by the luxury of the tours she conducted.

Material things are not very much important to me. I think as I got better and had something to eat and wasn't scared that I wouldn't get anything to eat, I think that was the only thing that I wanted to get in my life—to eat, then have something over my head, and that I didn't have to be scared. A roof over your head—it doesn't matter whether it's an apartment or a house, and it doesn't matter where it is.

The gorgeous house in Berlin; did she ever think she would live in such a place?

No, certainly not. My husband made that possible. But those things don't much matter to me now. What matters is if I have a roof over my head. I can live OK in a shack.

Proof of these sentiments is provided by what happened after she left Europe hurriedly to come to America to bury Brian. She brought a single piece of luggage, intending to return soon to Berlin. Everything else was left behind and was never re-trieved. The few personal photos pictured here she always car-ried with her; there are no others. Some people who lose their life possessions in a fire or other destructive act of nature or war suffer emotionally from that loss.   Their material life repre-sented their historical presence—a record of activities, values, accomplishments, changes, etc. It is no small matter to have all that snatched away. Millions of Jews as well as other victims of the war experienced such forfeiture and had to begin all over as Hannah did. She doesn't talk about the impact of losing what she left behind in the house in Berlin.

Although her social life is somewhat limited by choice, Hannah feels the important things in life include, after good health and a roof over your head . . .

> . . . *other people to love and to love you. Other people should be important in one's life. To have friends is a lot of work, and you have to take your friends as they are. They have to take me as I am, and that's a piece of work. You have to work at friendship every day. A friend needs to have the opportunity to talk to you about their lives. I have to have an opportunity to listen and let them speak, then take what I know about the subject and give back to them, because I'm a different person, with different perspective. That's how I get help—talk to friends about it, and I try to be a good listener.*

> *Today, sometimes I am very lonely. I am lonely that some-body talks to me, especially if I'm at home sick. Sometimes it hurts to be alone, but you have to get over that. You think if you had a partner or somebody to talk to, it would be easier to manage your life. But I don't want to have somebody that I just wash clothes and prepare food. I've*

been alone since 1967, and I adapted, but it's hard to be alone. I don't need excitement, I don't need money, and I don't need to go any place. I need to love, and I need people to love me.

Nobody gives a darn if you go around moping, no matter what the reason. And why do you need somebody to feel sorry for you? You think you are the only one who has a problem? I say get inside of yourself, get control of yourself and do something about it. Be strong and go ahead with your life. You don't need a counselor to tell you that. Too many people think when things go bad for them they have something coming in this world, but that's not what I think.

My concern is to be happy. I don't want any drama or sadness; I want to feel good inside. If I don't, I make myself feel good. A lot of people like to watch soaps or dramas with a lot of fighting, and I don't watch that. I'm going out of my way to keep conflict out of my life. At work I don't want any discussion about somebody is mad at somebody. If the news gets too much, I just turn it off. Not that I don't care about people, it's just something I don't want to feel. Maybe it's a selfish thing; I don't know. I'm trying to live my life positive.

Yes, I've survived some awful things. But the main thing that was taken away is somebody to care about me. I could have had somebody to love me, to be concerned about what happens to me like if I broke a leg or something. Maybe I could still have my house in Berlin. I miss all that; I really do. I would like somebody to take care of me, just for one day. I have always taken care of myself. When I got married, my husband took care of me for seven years. I waited for that all my life, but it wasn't possible any longer. So I had to get back into this thing again and take care of myself as well as my son.

I always had to be strong. Sometimes I just want to sit down and I don't want to be strong anymore. I'm tired of being strong. If only someone was there to say, 'I'll be strong for you.'

I assured her she gives strength to those around her. A close and meaningful relationship has developed between Hannah and Mark, a young friend in the community where she lives. He has become like a surrogate son, and she a mother figure to him. His own mother is deceased. Thus they each fill a void in the other's life, without the strings but with the blessings of affection and a feeling of accountability toward another human being.

Around her neck Hannah wears a delicate, almost inconspicuous gold chain with a few charms attached. She explained:

Memories are very important to me. Sometimes, if you love somebody you like to have a memory of this person on you, even if it's a piece of stone. Then that person is with me all the time. I confess to being a romantic; Wayne was too. I think that's how he got me after three dates; he was romantic to me.

Chapter Ten

HAVE WE LEARNED ANYTHING?

We ponder our own encounters with death,
weapons in hand,
and we weep silent tears
for those who waited
empty handed, for the
death blows to fall.
Death was the champion liberator,
not us, we saved but a few
at the very end,
and then we failed
as true avengers.

– Dee R. Eberhart
Excerpted from "Return Again" 1997
For a Shabbat service held in 1997 in Knoxville, TN.

Hannah is generous in her assessment of the German population's complicity in the extermination. From my own research, I would dispute that conclusion, but as a Jew living in postwar Germany, her observations have merit. For example, I noted that it was remarkable the nuns could send a Jew to the Olympics so soon after the war.

We were not announced as Jews. Nobody at that time would have thought about doing that. The nuns would never ever say anything . . . that 'we're housing Jews.' They did good things for us, but to admit there were Jewish kids in their convent, I don't think so. They were still scared, just like everybody else. That was still a bad time.

But at the Munich hospital where they recuperated after liberation, I reminded her, they knew these were Jewish children out of the camp.

Yes, but it was a special section of the hospital. At that time everybody was so glad the war was over. They knew from the newspapers, newsreels and whatever, what they did to the Jews, and they felt sorry for us. During the war some people felt for us; they liked us and wanted to help. But they needed to help themselves first. They couldn't fight, because they didn't have anything to fight with. I think at this point they were glad to do something for these leftover Jews. They knew they had done a lot that was wrong to the Jews, and they needed to do something right. The guilt trip of Germany was very large, especially while the Allies were there to remind them.

Older Germans did not like the Americans, or any of the Allied occupation forces for that matter. They lost their homes and cities in the bombing and their loved ones in the fighting. Younger girls liked the soldiers, because they offered an opportunity by marriage to leave that wrecked country.

Many people just distanced themselves from the Americans and didn't want to talk about what was done to the Jews. If you went to a party with people who went through the war and were soldiers, just regular soldiers who weren't Nazis, those soldiers were off fighting some place; they didn't know about the camps. The other part who were soldiers and also Nazis, they would say that was right what Hitler did. 'We needed to clean up Germany.' Another group would say, 'I'm going to keep out of this. I don't want to talk about it. I didn't know about this.' There are a lot of people in Germany my age or a little older, if they lived in a little small town somewhere, they probably didn't know anything about it. Anyway, that's generally what people would say for Americans.

There were Germans who knew and Germans who didn't know, and some just didn't comprehend what was going on.* They should have wondered where their Jewish neighbors were disappearing to, leaving the door of their house open. After the war nobody wanted to know. Even if they had compassion for us, who would go in there and help us out? Because you needed to live yourself. I could not expect anybody to go and get killed for me. There

*What Hannah says is true. But those communities and farms near camps saw the smoke, smelled the smell of death, used inmates as slave labor, and watched columns of the wretched on their death marches between camps toward the end of the war. Train station platforms were visible to all. Photos record the loading of deportees as well as police brutality of Jewish citizens on city streets.

*were people who would do that, and there were people who
didn't care, but I wouldn't blame them if they didn't. I
don't condemn those people for what they did or did not
do. When you're hungry, you'll walk over the dead Jews
to get something to eat. If I have a son or daughter and
I'm hungry with my kids, I don't know what I would do. I
haven't been in that position, so I can't talk about that.*

*I have actually been asked why the nuns didn't rescue us
sooner. I said, 'You question what those nuns did? What
could they have done?' I have always wondered why it
took so long for Allied troops to liberate the camps, why the
rest of the world didn't react to our plight sooner.*

Some Jewish children were safely hidden in convents during the war. Some Jewish families declined that option, however, because they did not want their children to be possibly
converted in that Catholic environment (although it could have
saved their lives). Non-Jewish families in many Nazi-occupied
countries temporarily provided foster homes for children, con-
cealing their true identities and presenting them as their own,
especially if they didn't look Jewish.

But the situation for children taken to a camp with their
parents was more likely unavoidable. Often the roundup for the
train-ride to a camp was swift and unexpected. A family might
not have time or proper contacts to provide for their children. At
the same time, there are some dramatic accounts in the literature of adolescents, even younger, who managed to avoid deten-
tion either for part of the war or entirely. They survived largely
on their own by a combination of good luck and sagacity beyond
their years.

Hannah and I discussed the Christian Church's negligence
and often overt anti-Semitism, which was evident in the writings

of certain Christians, even as they criticized the Nazi regime. It is well-established that anti-Semitism was not unique to Nazis or to Germany.

It took at least until 1970 to get this Jewish thing out of everybody, so they could say in their own German way 'Jude.' I wouldn't have said I was Jewish in Germany still in 1993. I was always scared. It might have changed since I been there. I was glad I didn't have a Jewish-sounding married name, and I don't look Jewish. I didn't have a problem because I never had to say I was Jewish, but I was always afraid.

I asked what would happen; would they shun you socially or fire you from your job?

No, it was just a personal thing, how you felt about it inside. Even my friends didn't know I was Jewish. No one ever saw me go to church or to synagogue in Germany.

Does Hannah consider herself Jewish?

I have Jewish heritage. Although I wasn't brought up as Jew, I will always be a Jew. When Brian was thirteen, we had to have this thing called 'bar mitzvah' to declare him to be a man. He had his bar mitzvah with Jewish friends, no other friends from the outside. After that, being Jewish was pretty much over for him.

Several Holocaust memoirs I have read were written by hunted people, not only Jews, who managed to escape internment by various means including assuming false identity. That strategy was not without its own set of dangers. For example, in Poland if you were a Pole, you could pretend to be German in order to protect yourself against the occupying Germans. But that made you suspect with the Poles if they didn't know you really weren't

German. There is an episode in Wladyslaw Szpilman's written memoirs, popularized in the movie *The Pianist*, in which he is almost shot by Polish citizens. They mistook him for a German when he appeared on the street wearing an overcoat given him by a German officer. If you were a Jewish Pole, you could pass yourself off as a Christian Pole, but that didn't save you from occupying Ukrainian troops, who ferociously annihilated Poles of any stripe and Germans as well. Hannah had her own take on that situation.

That's exactly the way I feel, and I think I have felt that way all my life. I have often felt I needed to be someone else. I would change my identity as soon as I felt everything wasn't kosher. Mostly in Germany, but sometimes in my travels. I had an interesting experience in Norway. We went on a cruise out of Rotterdam to Spitzbergen and Lofoten Island. We stopped at Geiranger Fjord, which was in Norway. We got into small boats and went in to the land just to look around, look at the houses, etc. I had twelve or thirteen people with me. As soon as those people knew we were from Germany, they took out their guns and got after us. Until I spoke English to them and said, 'I am an American!' I had to calm them down. They had so much hate for the Germans still in the '70s. They heard German talk and they were out there with their guns. Civilians off the street! I made myself clear that I was an American with an American passport, that these were just tourists. If I had been a German, we would have been in bad trouble, because they still hate Germans for what they did during the war. I bet if you took that same path today, you might have that same trouble.

Hannah disapproved of tracking down every last Nazi for

prosecution. It wasn't practical; it wasn't even possible, and so many years after the war—not very effective. She as well as her survivor friends felt there was a point to let go and get on with it. *"Why hang an 80-year-old man?"* Hannah cites some of the "professional" Holocaust spokesmen/activists as being bitter, sad old men. They admittedly have served a very useful purpose to society by not allowing the Holocaust to disappear from the collective conscience, but they are paying a high price by damaging their own outlook on life.

Why would you go through life like this? That is a very miserable life, I think. Nobody wants to know you if you're an angry person.

Knowing Hannah, it isn't surprising that she finds no fraternity in the gloominess of self-inflicted despair. She recognizes it is destructive to be immersed, however justifiably, in self-pity and anger over past injustice.

We discussed the good qualities that Germans traditionally bring to society. Author was raised among decent, hard-working, God-fearing German immigrants in Wisconsin and shares German heritage with millions of other Americans. No one can deny that wherever Germans settled in this country, they made it a better place by their industriousness, thrift, family values, and efficiency. Presently, author resides among similar citizenry in agricultural northern Colorado, many of whom are descendants of the Germans from Russia, or 'Volga Deutsche' as they are known locally. They came as stoop labor immigrants to the beet fields of northeastern Colorado during the decades straddling 1900. Today they own the land.

German traditional industriousness and organization went a long way in implementing the extermination strategy. They kept meticulous records at the camps, which after the war helped authorities sort out the fate of millions, as well as assisting individuals like Hannah who were looking for closure. The Nazis likely thought they would never be accountable for what they did. Why were they so organized in this particular endeavor?

That's the way Germans are, and I have some of that. In my office everything is organized, so that if anybody of any nationality came in there they could find everything. I would never have to explain anything.

Hannah is well aware German anti-Semitism is alive and well in some surprising places. At the Colorado motel, before she was manager, a German guest living in Canada arrived. Having identified each other as former German nationals, Hannah and this man conversed with each other. He admitted to being a former Nazi, apparently with no shame or regret, and made inappropriate claims about the "final solution." Hannah informed him she was a Jewish survivor of Dachau, and at this point the manager offered to throw him out. In her typical controlled, dignified manner, Hannah dismissed the incident. She did not think the issue or the guest was worth her anger or attention, and she simply exchanged no more words with him during his stay.

This was a disturbing incident to me as well, happening on home territory. In my naïveté because I live in "safe" northern Colorado, I assured Hannah that although there are some Americans who don't like Jews—an embarrassing truth I have to admit—it is a more benign anti-Semitism, if there is such a thing as "benign" anti-Semitism. It is rarely openly admitted in this era of political correctness and a far cry from the dangerous hostility promulgated by Nazi ideology. I would be surprised if such attitudes manifested themselves overtly or threatened Jews in our country, certainly not to promote putting anyone in a gas chamber. Hannah was quick to reply.

You don't know that. You have it here too. As much as you understand about my story, I know there are people in this country that think exactly like Hitler. I know that because I have come across it. I know where my mother-in-law lived in Idaho she lived very near where the white supremacists live. In Coeur d'Alene they had a supremacist parade! I heard things there I wouldn't have believed. I have met people in this country with ideas that scare me. I talked in a school in Montana, and there was a teacher who said to me after I had finished my talk, 'You know, what you just told me is all a lie.'

I said, 'I can prove what I said. Would you like me to prove it?'

His reply, 'Bullshit!'

I said, 'You don't have to believe it. Your principal invited me here to talk.' I found out later he was a member of the Ku Klux Klan.

You might not see them in your area, and you might not know them walking on the street, but they are in our American society. And there is still racism here. In 1962 when Wayne needed to go to Biloxi, Mississippi, I went with him for nine weeks. The Cuba crisis was going on. We lived in an apartment across from the Gulf of Mexico and saw missiles pointing out to the gulf. We saw the signs 'Colored enter here,' 'Whites enter here.' I couldn't understand that until somebody explained it. I couldn't fathom that they still had those problems in 1962.

As manager of a multi-ethnic staff, Hannah is keenly aware of human relations issues and the need for society to function without discrimination. She described a young man she has met in America who has a particularly vicious outlook toward minorities in general. To my question, "What makes people like that?" she replied, "*Parents.*" She also expressed concern about what young people are being exposed to or under-exposed to in their classrooms.

They don't care about what's good for their community or for society. They get caught up in their own macho thing, against-the-world, anti-establishment, belonging-to-a-group mentality. As a result, you don't say you're Jewish just any place. When I'm giving a talk, I've been asked to appear there, they know what to expect from me, and I know who I'm talking to. That's different. But I'm always uneasy, looking over my shoulder.

Hannah is sufficiently aware of the outrageous Holocaust Denial movement, which is as alarming as more overt anti-Semitic mentality. The very idea of denial is personally hurtful to Hannah and every other victim of the Holocaust. It is disturbing that denial is being promoted and disseminated on certain college campuses. Perhaps younger students are being exposed too. One wonders what the teacher in Montana said to his students after Hannah left the school.

People hear these things, like from the KKK, Louis Ferrakhan, white supremacists, and Neo-Nazis, and they believe them. They say that the pictures soldiers made of us are fake. The Nazis recorded everything about the people in the camps: names, birth dates, death dates, everything about them. It's there to read.

Another surprising twist to the post-Holocaust discussion pops up occasionally in the literature. It is in the form of questioning, even criticism, expressed by European Jews themselves as well as Israelis: why didn't Jews that were persecuted resist more? If they were going to be killed anyway, why didn't they take a guard or SS trooper down with them? Why didn't more of them join resistance groups? American servicemen as prisoners-of-war are instructed to continue resisting while confined, requiring the attention and resources of valuable enemy personnel and diverting those resources from other uses more critical to the war effort.

Bruno Bettelheim, noted child psychologist, emigrated to the US before WWII but spent time earlier at Dachau. He was critical of Anne Frank's family for secluding themselves in the expectation of carrying on a fairly normal, although restricted, pre-war life style. These condemning, unsympathetic criticisms present viewpoints with which I find it difficult to concur. In the end, what they are suggesting points to its own form of denial, that the Franks didn't take German aggression toward Jews seriously enough or that they rejected the reality of extermination by gas chambers.

A final episode confirms that Hannah has lost none of her spirit or her confidence, and that she considers herself an American patriot. The big stars and stripes flag she displays in her front yard announces that clearly enough.

When 9-11 happened, I was working in the motel. There was a recruiting station around the corner. When I heard what those planes did, I went to the recruiting officer that same day and asked him if I could enlist. He said I was too old. I wrote a letter to Washington D.C., and I said, 'If you don't need people like me because we are too old, then I don't think you are going to recruit anybody. I could do SOMETHING.'

That was a slap in my face. I didn't think they would say that. I was bold enough to believe the American Army or Air Force could use me. They don't have a draft anymore, and they don't have enough people. When something like 9-11 happens, you think we could do something. We just had an attack; we lost thousands of people, and that recruiter said I was too old. I was really offended and angry. And I told him so. He gave me an American flag, and I said, 'I have my own flag.' He should have called someone and said, 'We have someone here would like to enlist.'

I wanted to do that for my American son.

HAVE WE LEARNED ANYTHING?

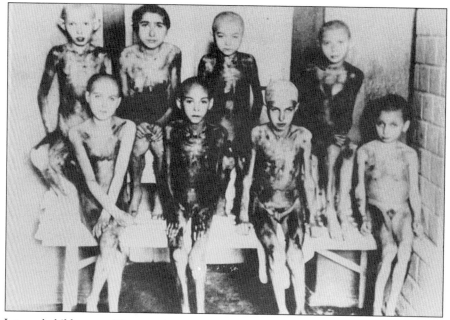

Interned children used for experiments.
Courtesy of United States Holocaust Memorial Museum.

Chapter Eleven

THE CAMP

When we first met,
we saw you and disbelieved.
You saw us and your joy overflowed,
as did our horror, rage and sorrow.
You who had forgotten how to cry,
wondered at our tears.

— Dee R. Eberhart

Excerpted from "When First We Met" 1993. Written for and presented
on Commemoration Day April 24, 1993 in Rotterdam, Netherlands at a
gathering of Dutch and European survivors of Dachau.

Dachau is a small town about ten miles northwest of Munich. The concentration camp of the same name was established in 1933 soon after Hitler came to power. The site was a former gunpowder factory vacated by terms of the 1918 Versailles Treaty which ended World War I. It was the first in the Nazi strategy to isolate and intern perceived political enemies of the state. In fact, it became a training ground for the SS engaged in the persecution of those individuals. SS effectiveness in the use of terror throughout the network of concentration and death camps that followed was developed at Dachau.

As more categories of "enemies" were identified and isolated, more camps were established to deal with them in Germany and throughout eastern Europe as the war progressed. Internees also came from other countries such as Poland, Czechoslovakia, the USSR, Romania, Hungary, Greece, and a surprising number were from France. At Dachau's liberation, only a minority of more than 30,000 living prisoners registered there were German. There were thousands more in Dachau's satellite camps and thousands who were moved in temporarily and unregistered, as Allied troops closed in. About 30% of the total were known to be Jewish. In fact, the majority of prisoners who died in the camp in its twelve-year existence were Catholic. The exact number of Jews who perished there is not known.

Dachau was not considered a death camp on the scale of such mass extermination centers as Auschwitz-Birkenau and Treblinka. To be sure, facilities were there for gassing, although it has been claimed they were not used for that purpose but as delousing showers. At any rate, the mortality rate was high. Inmates regularly lived on the edge of survival from many threats. But during the war, the camp and its subsidiaries served largely to provide a source of slave labor for the nearby armament factories and farms, as well as for medical experiments.

Adult inmates were also captive subjects for medical experimentation by the infamous Dr. Klaus Schilling.* Trials were conducted involving cures for TB, malaria, small pox, influenza, and other illnesses. Individuals would be artificially infected, then injected with serums, hoping to find cures for the disease (but not caring to cure the human guinea pig, of course).

Camp photos show internees suffering from the effects of experiments which subjected them to lack of oxygen. These tests were intended to determine how much oxygen deprivation German pilots could withstand at high altitudes. Some subjects died from these experiments. Dr. Sigmund Rascher, responsible for these and other brutal experiments at Dachau, was executed at the end of the war by his good friend and boss SS chief Heinrich Himmler.

There are discrepancies in descriptions about who was interned there, conditions, and procedures in general at Dachau. Even accounts of liberation of the camp by those who were there are controversial. Prisoners were moved from camp to camp, especially at the end of the war. In Hannah's case, she too may have spent some time in another camp. She does not remember being anywhere else but at Dachau. She is telling her story as she remembers it, and it is an honest account, burned into her consciousness. In my opinion, it doesn't matter where she received her tattoo or where she was abused. In the end, what is significant is the overall situation and that there is truth in the horror of it all despite inconsistency of details. And we give no quarter to the deniers.

Inmates were not the only victims of Dachau's horrors.

* Schilling was tried at Dachau as a war criminal, condemned, and hanged.

Liberation released the prisoners to whatever life they could resume, but American troops who took part in the liberation were also permanently affected by what they encountered there. Buchenwald was the first camp delivered by American forces, on April 11th; Dachau was the second. Stories had been filtering back to the Allies, but they were often dismissed as exaggerations, at the least simply unbelievable. Enlisted men and officers present at Dachau on April 29th received first-hand confirmation of the reality of the camp system. Troops of the famous 42nd "Rainbow" Division and the 45th "Thunderbird" Division of the Seventh Army were the first to witness these sights and confront their perpetrators. Some of these memories have been collected and published only within the last few years. Like many combat veterans as well as Holocaust survivors, there was reluctance if not downright unwillingness for many years to discuss that experience.

Copious regimental and personal accounts are available to the public in print and on the internet, offering details of the liberation of Dachau. All these recordings describe how seasoned combat troops on their way to take Munich were overwhelmed by what they unexpectedly discovered at the camp. Piles of dead bodies, emaciated and showing signs of beatings, were scattered around the premises. Equally horrifying were the barely-alive inmates who mobbed the troops—if they were able to get onto their feet—carrying their lice, TB, and typhus with them. Some rushed half-crazed to the barbed wire enclosing fence and were electrocuted, until power was turned off. Others tore some of the hated German guards apart with their bare hands. Troops reacted with rage, vomiting, crying, and an instinctive response to gun down some of the surrendering garrison. The camp commandant and his aides had already fled the scene.

Actually, if the rescuers had arrived one day later, Hannah and the other 30,000-plus prisoners would not have been alive to greet them. Reports revealed that Himmler had orders from Hitler that none of the internees be left alive in the face of imminent American occupation of the area. If there was not time to evacuate or eliminate them by "normal" procedures, they were to be fed poisoned soup or killed by gas released from the air. Fortunately, American advance was too swift to allow these orders to be carried out.

Within hours of the takeover, order was restored. Internees were kept inside the camp to provide for their welfare as well as to prevent them from seeking their own vengeance on the nearby countryside. Dachau townspeople were required to bury thousands of bodies found within the camp and in railway cars that had recently arrived transporting prisoners from other threatened camps. These cars were abandoned unemptied as the war came closer, sealing thousands of people to die just hours before liberation. When the doors were unlocked and the cargo was revealed, it was a scene never to be forgotten by those who witnessed it.

Present that day, Pfc. Dee Eberhart, I company, 242nd Infantry Regiment, made a sensitive and sobering observation when he wrote as a civilian in the 42nd Division's volume of collected memoirs.* Professor Eberhart reflected that "although the killing war was nearly over, the dying at Dachau would continue." And indeed it did, even months later in a convent orphanage in the nearby Bavarian Alps.

Immediate release of thousands of angry, sick, fragile, and homeless foreigners would have brought its own chaos. Field hospitals had to be set up immediately, the premises had to be

---

*Dachau 29 April 1945: The Rainbow Liberation Memoirs. See Consulted Works.

sanitized, and epidemics stemmed. Initially, even facilities for food storage and preparation to properly accommodate such numbers were lacking. These were unexpected challenges for the military forces in the area. Improved, the camp was used for several years after the war as a temporary residence for refugees.

Dachau imprisoned a number of VIPs, the names of which would be mostly unfamiliar to an overseas readership. Americans, however, will recognize the name of child psychologist Bruno Bettelheim. He was confined in 1938 and '39, released, then emigrated to the U.S.

Martin Niemoller, well-known as a Protestant theologian and anti-Nazi voice, was held at Dachau from 1941-45. After the war, his sentiments turned toward leniency for the war criminals and criticism of Allied efforts to prosecute them. Nevertheless, Pastor Niemoller's often quoted lines inspired by his camp experience carry an ominous message for all times.

Who will ever be free of Dachau?
Not the inmates who
somehow survived.
Not the Americans of '45.
Not the visitors who come to see.
Not the old guards with their secret thoughts.
Not the townsfolk of ancient Dachau.
Not Germany.
Not the rest of the world.
And not the spirits
who stand in rows
in the Appellplatz
waiting for the last transportcall,
or who stir the leaves of the memorial birch
and breathe gentle sighs
on the candles' flames.

– Dee R. Eberhart

Excerpted from "Herbertschausen" at a Russian Memorial Service in 1992.

FINAL THOUGHTS

No matter how long you live, just when you think you have seen it all, something still more wonderful or terrible enters your consciousness to shock you once again. Such has been my privilege to know and work with Hannah. I experienced both extremes, and I'm sure I will never be the same. At the same time, I hope knowing Hannah's story will penetrate the heart and soul of all who read it, in the way Anne Frank's diary did so many years ago. Unlike Anne, with the benefit of longevity Hannah's life story is reminding us to go out and live life as we never have before, before it's too late. Love, help others, forgive, laugh, be grateful, share, sing and dance, love some more—and NEVER forget the events that inspired this narrative.

TOPICS FOR THOUGHT AND DISCUSSION

1. What did you learn about the Holocaust that you didn't already know? What surprised you?

2. Can you put yourself into the position of Hannah's family? In the 1930s with all the signs of trouble, would you leave Germany or stay?

3. Would you surrender three-year-old Hannah or your own child to others, possibly strangers, for her protection until the "emergency" was over? Keep in mind that parents who sent their children to England, Canada, or the US could be fairly confident they would be safe and reunited with the family after the war was over.

4. How would you react to being routed out of your house or apartment, allowed to take a small suitcase of belongings with you, not knowing if you would ever return to reclaim ownership?

5. Would you resist? How would you resist? If you haven't experienced military training, could you as a law-abiding, moral citizen kill your oppressors?

6. Can you imagine yourself having enough will, determination, faith, and purpose as Viktor Frankl describes, to endure years of hardship as a slave laborer or prisoner?

7. What would your goal be? How would it change at different stages in your life? As an adolescent, young adult, mature adult?

8. How would you mobilize your determination to triumph over your ordeal? Would it be faith, anger, simple hope that someday it had to end?

9. Would you succumb to stealing from your fellow inmates, serving as an informer, or otherwise ensuring better treatment, perhaps survival, for yourself? Differently for a loved-one?

10. Could you forgive and make the peace that Hannah has?

11. Would your personal experience as well as the entire Holocaust alter your religious views? Some people ask, "Where was God during the Holocaust?" What is your opinion?

12. Would you live in postwar Germany as Hannah did, looking over your shoulder, not having a support system?

13. Will this story of Hannah affect your future behavior, your values, your relationships? How?

CONSULTED WORKS

Bitton-Jackson, Livia. *I Have Lived a Thousand Years*. New York: Simon and Schuster Books for Young Readers, 1997. An adolescent Hungarian's wartime experience, including graphic description of camp life at Auschwitz.

Buechner, Col. Howard, M.C. AUS (Ret.). *Dachau: The Hour of the Avenger*. Metairie, LA: Thunderbird Press, 1988. A well-written, thorough description of Dachau liberation. Buechner, a medical doctor and eye-witness himself, addresses the contradictory and controversial accounts by other sources. Highly recommended reading.

Dann, Sam. Editor. *Dachau 29 April 1945: The Rainbow Liberation Memoirs*. Lubbock: Texas Tech University Press, 1998. A volume of individual troop accounts.

Eberhart, Dee R. *Illusions: World War II Poems*. Harrisburg, Oregon: The Saurus Press, 2004. Excerpted poems reprinted by permission of the author.

Encyclopedia of the Holocaust. New York: MacMillan, 1990.

Frankl, Viktor. *Man's Search for Meaning*. New York: Washington Square Press/Simon and Schuster, 1985. First published in Austria in 1946, this celebrated Austrian psychotherapist served his own time in Auschwitz. From his camp experiences, he devised his theories into what is recognized as "logotherapy." A classic of Holocaust literature.

Gun, Nerin E. *The Day of the Americas*. New York: Fleet, 1966. Only a portion describes the Dachau liberation as related by Gun, a former inmate of the camp. The rest recounts events after the war relating to resettlement of refugees, etc. Gun was a Turkish journalist jailed by the Nazis.

Gold, Alison Leslie. *Fiet's Vase*. New York: Jeremy P. Tarcher/Penguin, 2003. Collection of stories from different survivors.

Goldhagen, Daniel Jonah. *Hitler's Willing Executioners: Ordinary Germans and the Holocaust*. New York: Vintage Books (Random House), 1996.

Greene, Joshua M. *Justice at Dachau: The Trials of an American Prosecutor*. New York: Broadway Books, 2003. Survey of trials of German war criminals from American-occupied military zone, held at Dachau 1945-48.

I Never Saw Another Butterfly . . . New York: McGraw-Hill, no date. Collection of children's drawings and poems from Terezin concentration camp in Czechoslovakia 1942-44.

Immell, Myra H. Editor. *Readings on the Diary of a Young Girl*. San Diego: Literary Companion Series, Greenhaven Press, 1998. Essays examining issues raised in Anne Frank's diary.

Lace, William W. *The Death Camps*. San Diego: Lucent Books, 1998. One volume of Lucent's concise, amply-illustrated, easily-read series *The Holocaust Library*.

Lagnado, Lucette Matalon, and Sheila Cohn Dekel. *Children of the Flames: Dr. Josef Mengele and the Untold Story of the Twins of Auschwitz.* New York: William Morris, 1991.

Lifton, Robert Jay. *The Nazi Doctors: Medical Killing and the Psychology of Genocide.* New York: Basic Books, 1986.

Lipstadt, Deborah. *Denying the Holocaust: The Growing Assault on Truth and Memory.* New York: Free Press (MacMillan), 1993.

Lobel, Anita. *No Pretty Pictures: A Child of War.* Greenwillow Books, New York: 1998.

Marcuse, Harold. *Legacy of Dachau,* Cambridge: Cambridge University Press, 2001.

Nir, Yehuda. *The Lost Childhood.* New York: Scholastic Press, 2002. An unusual, well-written, and inspiring survival account of a Polish Jewish adolescent, his mother, and sister, who stayed out of the camps by deception. A five-star recommendation.

Notowitz, David. *Voices of the Shoah: Remembrances of the Holocaust.* Los Angeles: Rhino Entertainment, 2000. Four CDs and accompanying, illustrated book. Described as an audio-documentary with complete transcripts of interviews conducted by Elliott Gould.

Rice, Earle, Jr. *The Final Solution.* San Diego: Lucent Books, 1998. Another volume of Lucent's series *The Holocaust Library.*

Sparks, General (Ret.) Felix. 157th Infantry Regiment, 45th Infantry "Thunderbird" Division, Seventh US Army. Personal memoirs, Lakewood, CO: 1989.

Szpilman, Wladyslaw. *The Pianist.* New York: Picador, 1999. Another personal account, by a Polish musician who managed to avoid Nazi camps.

Warren, Andrea. *Surviving Hitler: A Boy in the Nazi Death Camps.* New York: Harper Trophy (Harper Collins Publishers), 2002. Jack Mandelbaum, a Polish teen-ager, spends three years in the camps, including Auschwitz. Well-told, gripping story for young readers but appropriate for adults as well.

Wiesel, Elie. *Night.* New York: Bantam Books edition for Hill and Wang, 1982. One of the best-known Holocaust survivors recounts his experiences as a teenager in several camps. Wiesel has written much about the Holocaust.

NOTES

Share your thoughts with other readers.

NOTES